LOVETT F. EDWARDS

METHUEN & CO LTD
II NEW FETTER LANE EC4

*The church of Sv. Jovan Bogoslov
(Kaneo) on the lake of Ohrid*

First published 1954
Second edition 1967
© 1967 *by Lovett F. Edwards*
Printed and bound in Great Britain
by C. Tinling & Co Ltd, Liverpool and Prescot

77274

Contents

Foreword to Second Edition

Ten years is a long time in a rapidly developing country like Yugoslavia. This has meant considerable revision of the earlier edition of this book, much of which was written many years ago. New towns have been built which did not exist before and many of the older ones have been completely transformed. The standard of living has improved greatly, especially in the villages, and each federal capital has become a minor metropolis.

This has inevitably led to a certain loss of the picturesque. A village of neat, new houses, almost always with electric light and often with running water, is less attractive to the visitor than its wide-eaved, tumbledown predecessor. But it is a far more comfortable place in which to live. National costumes and national songs still exist, though they are harder to find. Many of the mediaeval churches and monasteries have become museums; this makes them less romantic but has ensured their continued existence. The work of preservation has been carefully and reverently carried out. Without this government aid, many of them would by now have become mere heaps of rubble and their wonderful frescoes smoke-blackened walls.

Therefore it is well to avoid too great a feeling of nostalgia when writing of Yugoslavia. On the whole, the changes have been for the better. Certainly multi-storey hotels do not improve the Dalmatian landscape, but they do make it possible for the average person to enjoy it; and there is still plenty of savage and untamed nature for the traveller anxious to get off the beaten track.

Yugoslavia is a country pulling itself upward by its own bootstraps, and it is making a very good job of it. Progress is rapid and inevitable. There is a tremendous stress on industrialization, but this is common to all countries today.

The visitor has, indeed, every reason to be satisfied. Hotels are many and, on the whole, comfortable, though standards of service can still be improved. Ancient monuments and works of art have been scrupulously preserved. National traditions have been jealously fostered and are still alive, even though sometimes with a slight smack of artificiality. This sounds carping and critical, but is not so intended. If a fine thing is dying it is good to keep it alive, even if it has no longer the full vigour of youth. A country is not a museum and cannot be expected to look like one for the benefit of the occasional traveller.

These changes are the result of two irresistible forces: the pace of reconstruction after the ravages of the last war, which were worse in Yugoslavia than in any other country, save perhaps Poland or western Russia, and the enormous pressure of modern economics. Young people want to make their way in the world, to be 'with it'.

But the natural beauty and grandeur of the country remain and have become far more accessible. Furthermore, the kindness and hospitality of the people (and in this I include even the officials) is still very much alive. The harshness and suspicion of the immediate post-war years has gone. The traveller feels himself a welcome guest.

This book is intended for the intelligent visitor to Yugoslavia. Therefore I have concentrated largely on those parts of the country he is most likely to see, that is to say the Adriatic coast, Slovenia, Montenegro and Bosnia. I shall have much to say also about Belgrade and Zagreb and about the mediaeval cities and monasteries of Serbia and Macedonia, now once more open to the visitor. It is worth travelling across all Europe to see the lake and city of Ohrid.

That is not to say that other parts of Yugoslavia are without interest. The racial and historical chequerboard of the Voivodina is a most fascinating study. There is space there and sky. But the area has few tourist attractions and one must have friends there to be able to love and understand it. The trip through the Danube gorges is one of the most dramatic and colourful in the world. East Serbia and south-eastern Macedonia are also interesting places, but the communications are poor and there is little or no accommodation for the visitor. I have, therefore, left them out.

I have tried to concentrate on those things that have endured despite changes of government and ideology. Therefore I have avoided details of prices and accommodation that vary year by year and may be out of date even before a book of this size can be printed. I have also avoided politics; there are countless books and periodicals on this subject for those who want them.

Note on the pronunciation of Yugoslav names

In this book I have made no attempt to anglicize Yugoslav proper names, with the exception of Belgrade (Serbo-Croat – Beograd) and Yugoslavia (Serbo-Croat – Jugoslavija) which would seem absurd to an English reader in their proper form.

In Istria I have given the Slav names, which are admittedly less known than their Italian equivalents. However, these are the names used in the country itself.

I have used the Latin Croatian forms throughout. Slovene has the same phonetics and the same alphabet, Serbian the same phonetics but the Cyrillic alphabet.

There are a certain number of minor variations from the Serbian Cyrillic in the newly recognized Macedonian language, which was finally established in 1945. Therefore some of the Macedonian names differ slightly from the forms used in the earlier edition of this book – e.g. Bitola for Bitolj.

Serbian and Croatian are practically the same, with slight dialect differences with which it is unnecessary to worry the reader. Slovene is different but with similar orthography so that one need anticipate no difficulties. All the south Slav dialects are mutually comprehensible, although sometimes embarrassing misunderstandings can arise.

Serbo-Croat is strictly phonetic. One sound is always designated by one letter, or combination of letters; in the Cyrillic alphabet always by a single letter. The foreigner cannot go far wrong if he uses 'continental' vowels and English consonants, with the following exceptions:

   c is always *ts* as in cats. Example: Car – Tsar. *ica* is a common geographical ending, e.g. Planica – Planitsa, or Crikvenica – Tsrikvenitsa.

   č is *ch* as in church. Example: Čačak – Chachak.

ć is similar but softer, as *t* in the Cockney pronunciation of tube. Most Serbian and many Croatian and Slovene family names end in *ć*. In the everyday spoken language there is little difference between *č* and *ć*, and for practical purposes the foreigner may regard them as the same.

dj is the English *j* in jam – the English *j* in fact. In Cyrillic it is a single letter.

dž is practically the same, but harder. It is usually found in words of Turkish origin, e.g. džamija – mosque. In Cyrillic it is a single letter.

j is always soft, the English *y*. Example: Jugoslavija – Yugo-slavi(y)a. After *n* or *l* it merely softens those consonants, without being pronounced separately, as in news. Example: Ulcinj. In the Cyrillic alphabet *nj* and *lj* are single letters.

š is *sh* as in shake. Example: Sušak – Sushak.

ž is *zh* as *z* in azure. Example: Župa – Zhupa; cf. French *j* in jamais.

There are no double letters in Serbo-Croat.

The stress is usually on the penultimate syllable; never on the final syllable

A map of
YUGOSLAVIA

In the Postojna Caves

CHAPTER I

Istria – The Fantastic Karst

Ode to the north-east wind – Underground rivers and caverns of the karst – Languages – Yugoslav roads – The Magistrale – The Kvarner Riviera – Poreč and Piran – The fortress-churches of Istria.

Since the war the Yugoslav frontiers have moved westward and, despite the protestations of the purists, are likely to remain more or less as they are today. The result has been to leave long-disputed Istria in Yugoslav territory.

Many visitors to Yugoslavia approach this way. It has been the classical invasion route since – or even before – the days of the Roman Empire. More practically and immediately, it is the easiest route by car from western Europe and the route of the Simplon Orient Express.

As soon as the train leaves Trieste and commences spiralling upwards towards the frontier station of Sežana there are signs that one is entering a new country. The first of these is a series of tremendous stone walls, many feet thick, flanking the more exposed sections of the track. Travellers accustomed to northern Europe or the United States immediately think of them as snow barriers and wonder why they are not roofed and how there can be so much snow in this land, as they look down over the brilliant blue of the Adriatic.

In fact, they are not. They are wind-breaks. For as the train enters Istria, it enters the land of the bura, the terrible north-east wind that, starting in the steppes, chilled by the Carpathians and gathering force across the wide Danubian plain, piles up against the masses of the Julian Alps and the Dinaric ranges and then bursts out in fierce and destructive squalls down the narrow mountain valleys leading to the Adriatic and the Kvarner Gulf. It blows, sometimes for days on end, in the winter and early spring,

17

rendering navigation in the Kvarner (Quarnero) exceedingly dangerous at these times. The rails around the sea-front corners in Trieste are not, as the summer visitor might imagine, to protect the incautious jay-walker from the Triestine traffic. They are to give him some support to hold on to when the bura is blowing. The bura causes immense destruction and at times is violent enough to derail a train.

On the first occasion when I heard this, I thought it was a traveller's tale. But I took the trouble to check the records and found that it actually happened on at least three occasions, though admittedly not recently and not near Trieste. Twice it occurred on the hairpin bends leading down to the harbour at Rijeka and once on the narrow-gauge railway from Sinj to Split in central Dalmatia. On the Danubian plain and in Belgrade this terrible wind is known as the košava – 'the mower'.

However in summer and autumn the bura blows less frequently and less violently and is unlikely to trouble the holiday-maker. Its extreme force in winter is due to the sudden change in temperature between the snow-covered heights and the warmth of the coastlands. In summer, when these differences are slight, it is a cooling and refreshing breeze and often very welcome. The peasants watch the summits of the Istrian Alps and the Velebit. When these are wreathed in cloud the bura is due.

At Sežana you enter fully into the karst. This word karst – carso, kras, krš – comes from a Celtic root and means, appropriately enough, 'stony'. But it has come to be applied, by geologists and travellers, to a special kind of rock formation, typical of Istria, Dalmatia and Montenegro, which extends southwards into Albania and Greece and is also to be found in the heel of Italy, Puglia. Its peculiar forms dominate not only the landscape but also the history and way of life of the whole of the eastern Adriatic. It is characteristic and inescapable. But its desolate wildness adds a greater charm by contrast to the little fertile poljes (plains) and the old cities by the sea-coast.

It is a vast stretch of limestone rock, bare and porous, so that it holds little earth and less water. It is almost impossible to scratch a living out of it, for the forests that once held the soil precariously in place were long ago felled by Turks or Venetians and what they left the goats destroyed. The goats have, indeed, been more destructive than the armies, but now, I am glad to see, the Yugoslav state is waging war on them. I do not know the precise law about goats, but it seems they may only be kept in limited numbers and under control; the former rapacious herds that laid bare the hill-sides have disappeared. As a result many of the once stony hillsides are being covered by young forest, often scrub oak, which not only makes them more beautiful but which will, eventually, improve the water supply and moderate the climate. It is an achievement of which to be proud.

The karst is fantastically honeycombed by huge caves and ghylls, where the rivers appear and disappear at will. Many spring full-grown out of the rocky hillside, while their upper courses wind darksomely among the mountain caverns, often impossible to trace.

The soil, such as it is, is collected into tiny pockets among the stones, known as vrtače, too shallow for the plough, which may yield a few ears of maize only after long and painful labour with the hoe. The few towns or villages of the inland karst are situated on the poljes, which are for the most part river valleys where there is soil and water, and these make up for the barrenness of the land by an extraordinary fertility. Sometimes these rivers are seasonal, flooding the poljes in spring till they become vast lakes and dis-appearing in summer into ghylls, or ponors, to continue their course mysteriously underground until the melting snows force them once more to the surface. This accounts for the diverse tales of travellers, especially on the road from Dubrovnik to Mostar and Sarajevo. Some speak of immense lakes, where others, only a few months later, will find only a trickle of water and broad acres of corn or stunted maize or the mathematically exact lines of the tobacco plants. How the inhabitants of the more distant villages contrive to scrape a living is a mystery, but they are among the most vigorous and hardy of the Yugoslavs and make some of the finest soldiers in the world. Mostly they have big families and in the days when America was a free country used to emigrate in large numbers. Now they are among the chief sources of energy of the Yugoslav state.

The sparse, rocky soil is especially good for wine and for olives and figs, which are among the staple products of Dalmatia, and the people make use of the few plants which grow naturally in the interstices of the stones: wild asparagus, pomegranates, and all manner of medicinal and culinary herbs, such as capers, salvia, rosemary and pyrethrum.

Along the sea-coast, however, the karst is kindlier. Exceedingly rocky, with countless small harbours and deep fjords extending far into the mainland, it is the most diversified coastline of southern Europe. Down as far as Montenegro it is protected by a chain of islands, themselves outcrops of the karst, which shelter the sea-coast cities usually built on river estuaries or where some more fertile valley reaches the sea. These sea-born poljes are larger and richer than those inland, and it was on them that the maritime cities of Istria and Dalmatia developed. Cut off by geography and also often by politics from their hinterland, these cities looked seaward, relying on trade and not infrequently piracy for their wealth. Save for Dubrovnik, they were seldom strong enough to stand alone, but managed for many centuries to preserve a local independence not seriously interfered with by their distant overlords. Distance: that was the key – distance and trade. So that in the centuries-old struggle between the mainland and the maritime powers they chose the latter, who interfered less with their affairs and allowed them to preserve some at least of their trade and municipal privileges.

Thus, in the cities, cultural and social influences came from across the sea, from Greece, Rome, Byzantium and the Italian maritime republics, above all Venice; in the countryside from the dominant land-power, Rome, Byzantium, Serbia, Bosnia, Croatia, the Turks or the Hungarians. After the fall of Venice the mainland influence predominated and the whole area sank into more than a century of profound stagnation under the Austro–Hungarian monarchy, which feared the growing influence and numbers of the Slavs and tried, unsuccessfully, to bolster up the Italian influences on the sea-coast in all save politics. The travels of T. G. Jackson in the eighties tell a sorry story of dirt, desolation, decadence and decay. Only the union of the sea-coast with its hinterland, and the development of modern communications after the First World War, saved the cities of Dalmatia from becoming mouldering and seldom-visited museum pieces. The racial pressure of the Slavs, growing in force through the centuries, completed the work. Dalmatia today, though still proud of her ancient Latin cultural tradition, is, save for Serbia and Montenegro, the most Slav of the regions of Yugoslavia. Istria, nearer to Italy and with a larger Italian minority, has had to wait for its liberation until recent years, after the Second World War. Here the process of consolidation is still incomplete, but there is little doubt that it will take the same course.

The process is still going on. After years of uncertainty and deferred plans, a beginning has been made on two more big projects to link the coast with the interior and this has meant the development of two new ports: Bar, and Ploče on the Neretva estuary. Bar has now direct car-ferry connections with Bari in Italy and a railway line to Titograd which will eventually be continued to Belgrade. Ploče is still mainly in the planning stage but has even greater possibilities. The railway line to Sarajevo is now open.

One of the minor results of the new frontiers has been the revival of interest in Postojna. Under the Austro–Hungarian monarchy the huge Postojna caverns (or Postumia or Adelsberg – almost all these towns have three names, according to language) were a place of pilgrimage for our Victorian grandfathers, who wandered among their vast stalactite growths and looked with awe at the sources of the river Pivka roaring beneath. These caves are one of the most impressive fantasies of the karst. Their full extent has never been completely ascertained but some twenty kilometres have been explored, while about half this has been rendered accessible and is reasonably easy to see by judicious cat-walks, electric light and even, for a short stretch, an underground electric railway.

It is probable that our grandfathers' taste for the Gothic has been greatly modified by the outspokenness and cynicism generated by two world wars, and it can have done little harm to Postojna to have been relatively deserted for over twenty years. For between the wars Postojna was a frontier station and visitors were generally too concerned with passport and customs formalities to try to visit caverns, however famous.

The tamed magnificence of Postojna may seem very trite to the modern speleologist, for whom there are almost equally extensive, but not so well-known, caverns at Škocjanska Jama, near the present frontier station of Sežana. In fact the whole Istrian watershed develops underground and its mountains are honeycombed with galleries.

These pot-holes have the local name of foibe and earned an unenviable reputation during the last war as a convenient way for disposing of prisoners. One of them, at Basovica near Trieste, was once carefully examined to try and assess the responsibility for this jacquerie. But the report on it, if ever written, does not seem to have been published. When I talked with one of the soldiers assigned to this unpleasant task, he said that it was almost impossible to know which of the many occupying fascist, nazi or quisling forces bore the greatest responsibility. All of them seemed to have made use of the foibe, and all of them bound the hands and feet of their victims with pilfered telegraph wire. Order was only restored after the victory of the partisan forces.

The story of a young Slovene partisan who managed to free his limbs after he had been thrown into this natural charnel-house and escape by swimming through the underground water-channels has become the subject of one of those interminable ballads that are passed from mouth to mouth, despite the ravages of the written word, and can still be heard occasionally in the more remote mountain villages.

The present federal administration of Yugoslavia has blunted many of these inter-tribal rivalries and today there is little of the fierce hatreds formerly existent between Serbs, Croats and Macedonians. The new Yugoslav man is still being forged, but the process is peaceful. Istria is on a linguistic frontier and is now divided between the federal republics of Slovenia and Croatia. Roughly speaking, the Slovenes live in the mountains and the Croats, and what remains of the Italian minority, on or near the coast. The small group of Rumanian-speaking villages at the foot of Mt. Učka (Monte Maggiore) in the Valdarsa region is an ethnic curiosity. They have had no contact with modern Rumania and are more likely to be allied with such late Latin remnants as the Romansch- and Ladino-speaking peoples.

Language is an important matter for the visitor. For a short time after the war Russian was taught in the Yugoslav schools as a second language for ideological reasons. It posed a lot of problems for the teachers, since the two languages are etymologically and morphologically similar, but their pronunciation and accentuation are completely different and the common words most in use differ greatly and can easily give rise to amusing and embarrassing contretemps. To ask for a match in Russian comes very close to a gross indecency in Serbo-Croat.

Since Marshal Tito's break with the Cominform, English has become the second language in Yugoslav schools. It is also being widely studied by older people. Thus it is not, as a rule, very difficult to find someone in every town who can speak some English. In the coastal cities, and especially on the islands, there are also many sailors and returned emigrants to lend a helping tongue, though their vocabulary often smacks somewhat of the docks or the factories. German is a useful language in Croatia.

Serbo-Croat is itself a beautiful language and the easiest of the Slav tongues, though this should not be regarded too optimistically; all the Slav tongues are difficult. I do not advise anyone to try Slovene; it is philologically fascinating because of its archaic forms, but a good deal more difficult. Besides, almost every Slovene knows some Serbo-Croat, whereas the opposite is not always the case. Serbo-Croat bears roughly the same relation to Russian as Spanish to Italian; it is a stronger, harsher, more sonorous and masculine speech. Macedonian is even harsher, and was only standardized as a literary language after the war; but of that more in its place.

Before leaving the question of language, it is worth remarking that both Serbian and Croatian – usually referred to under the composite form Serbo-Croat – are two dialects of the same language though with some amusing minor differences, as between English and American. This is not always obvious to the visitor, as Serbian is written in Cyrillic characters and Croatian in Latin letters with a number of diacritic signs. For those who want to travel farther from the coast it is worth while learning the Cyrillic letters. The alphabet is not hard to learn and has the advantage of being strictly phonetic. Macedonian also uses Cyrillic letters, with a few local modifications.

But to return to Istria. In the coastal towns a good deal of Italian is still spoken and many public notices are in both Slovene (or Croatian) and Italian.

One of the benefits remaining from Italian rule – the Istrians are inclined to say that they were very few – is good road maintenance. Even in Albania the Italian occupiers left good roads behind them, though in this case the local authorities soon dissipated their inheritance by neglect. However, in Istria the main roads are good and the smaller ones, though narrow and precipitous, usually have a metalled surface.

This cannot be said of Yugoslav roads as a whole. Those in Slovenia are usually good, but in other parts of the country they still leave a good deal to be desired. Their condition usually depends on the local road-building material available. None the less, much has been done and, little by little, the main centres are being linked by a system of motor-roads. These are good, though the term motor-road usually merely means that they cannot be used by peasants carts or pedestrians (this rule is often ignored in Macedonia). One main system runs right through the country from the frontier to Ljubljana and Zagreb, on to Belgrade, and then on to Niš and the Bulgarian frontier to the east, and Gevgelija (frontier station with Greece) to Salonica in the south. This is gradually being linked up to the main cities of Macedonia, but the motorist must take care. The new roads are excellent, but then suddenly there may be a long stretch not yet rebuilt where the road surface is bad. In Dalmatia the main coastal road will have been completed by the time this book appears. It is good and very spectacular, running the whole way to Ulcinj in the extreme south, with a new branch linking it to Titograd, the capital of Montenegro. But landslides are frequent, so that longish stretches are almost always being repaired, and high speeds are inadvisable. It is known as the Magistrale.

Generally speaking, the excellent Yugoslav road-map should be read by English motorists with a discount of at least one grade for every road rating. Standards differ and there is a good deal of healthy optimism among Yugoslav cartographers. For journeys off the beaten track a mule or a jeep is recommended.

However, from Rijeka an excellent road leads along the

western shore of the Kvarner (Quarnero) Gulf. It passes, one after the other, three well-known seaside resorts – Opatija (Abbazia), Lovran and Mošćenička Draga. Their popularity is in that order; their charm, in my opinion, is in the reverse. But then I am one of those who strongly object to the 'development' of seaside resorts. Their charm should derive from their natural position and the beauty left them by the centuries. Development should limit itself to cleanliness and tidiness and the provision of suitable – not necessarily luxurious – accommodation. Far too many horrors are committed in the magic name of tourism.

Opatija is, to my mind, over-developed. Its numerous hotels, restaurants, bars (in Yugoslavia the word bar usually means a cabaret) and dance-halls remind me of such places as Nice, Brighton or Blackpool and do not suit the wild beauty of the Kvarner. Despite the comparative austerity of present-day Yugoslavia, Opatija still reflects the flashy and meretricious taste of the Magyars who were its principal visitors before the First World War.

This is a personal opinion, and I know that there are many who will not agree with me. The sort of attractions that Opatija has to offer may easily be found nearer home, and Yugoslavia has more beautiful and fascinating places. Opatija is, however, a centre for frequent displays of Yugoslav folk-music and dancing. These are magnificent and provide a striking introduction to the beauties of the land. Admittedly such things are far more beautiful and impressive in their natural setting, yet it would take many years of residence and many miles of travelling to hear and see so many of them so well done.

Lovran, a mile or so down the road, is charming. Development has gone just far enough. There are excellent hotels, which do not encroach overmuch on the natural beauties of the Gulf. My own taste is for Mošćenička Draga, another mile or so down the road.

I do not propose to go into details about hotels. Their number and quality change from year to year. The Yugoslav government publishes a hotel guide which can be relied upon. The Yugoslavs are not as a rule slick hoteliers of the Swiss or Italian type, but they are friendly and helpful, especially to visitors from England or America. Younger people, who do not mind a rougher and semi-communal existence, will have an excellent time in the many hostels, 'campings', workers' camps and so forth. Their companions will be hospitable, good-natured and friendly, even if a trifle over-curious, by English standards, about one's personal affairs. But this is a characteristic of all south-east Europe and arises out of real interest and not mere 'nosiness'.

Older people, however, will do better at the hotels.

Even here, there should be a word of warning. The standard grows better year by year, but the hordes of tourists anxious to spend their summers in Dalmatia have strained the Yugoslav hotel industry to the utmost. New and luxurious hotels are going up month by month and most of them are very good. But, as a Montenegrin official remarked to me, it is easy to put up a magnificent tourist object; the difficulty is to staff it. Frequently the staff is recruited from local peasants who are not used to the comforts of Class A hotels. They do not always realize that the visitor demands a higher standard, with which they are not familiar. A few spots on a tablecloth mean nothing to a peasant, who often cannot understand what all the fuss is about. In the interior this may also apply to plumbing and sanitary fittings. The officials responsible are only too well aware of this and are far more worried about obtaining suitable staff than about erecting smart new hotels, of which there are perhaps too many already.

But this digression has taken us far from Istria, where the hotels are, as a rule, very good.

The cities of the western Istrian coast have a very ancient history. Pula, for example, claims to have been founded by the Colchians after the dramatic voyage of the Argonauts. Indeed the very name of Istria may be an echo of that distant adventure.

In historical times the Istrian cities were more unlucky than their Dalmatian fellows. They were nearer the centres of power, both by sea and land, and thus were unable to preserve their municipal independence for so long. After the break-up of the Roman Empire they remained for a time under the Byzantine Exarchate of Ravenna, and upon its downfall in 752 passed to the Lombard Kingdom. It is difficult to condense the extremely crowded and complicated history of two millennia into as many sentences, but when all central power was finally abolished they became for more than a thousand years mere pawns in the game of local power politics between the Patriarchate of Aquileia, the Marquises (later Counts) of Istria, the Italian maritime republics and, above all, the Most Serene Signoria of Venice. In addition there were continual raids by the Uskok pirates of Dalmatia, and almost every city, to make confusion worse confounded, was torn by internal factions, the populace siding mainly with Venice and the nobles with their various feudal overlords, later to be fused into the Hapsburg Empire.

Of all these rivals the Republic of Venice was the most powerful, since it could control the sea-borne trade by which the cities lived. But Venice was none too eager to take over responsibility in Istria; for many years, indeed centuries, it was content that the cities remained *fideles*, paid tribute and contributed to the Venetian fleets. It was not until the thirteenth century that they became *subjectos*. For this voluntary subjection they were sacked and destroyed, not for the first or last time, by the Genoese in the following century, during the war of Chioggia.

What wars, revolutions and factions had begun, piratical raids and pestilence finished. Several times in its history Istria was almost depopulated. In the sixteenth and early seventeenth centuries Pula, whose population in Roman and again in modern times topped the thirty thousand mark, was reduced to three hundred souls, Poreč (Parenzo) was left with one hundred, and the few remaining local boys are said to have amused themselves by snaring birds in the central square of their city. Smaller cities were completely deserted.

Immigrants and refugees from the Turkish invasions were called in to fill the gap. We hear of great settlements of Slavs from Bosnia, Hercegovina, Dalmatia and even Montenegro summoned by Venice on frequent occasions to people the deserted countryside. These invitations continued from 1376 until the end of the seventeenth century. From time to time the citizens of the towns would protest against these newcomers, claiming that they were wild and uncultivated, as at that time they probably were, so that their settlements were limited to the barren karst, where Slav settlers had existed since the Dark Ages. But the towns themselves were equally depopulated, so immigrants were brought in from more civilized regions, such as parts of Greece, Crete and from all over the Levant, until little or no trace of the original Thracian, Celtic or Roman townspeople was left.

The Roman-Byzantine tradition of the cities remained, strongly fortified by centuries of Venetian rule. But in view of this long and troubled history, ethnological arguments about the Istrian cities based on race are not only pretentious but demonstrably stupid. All that can matter is who lives there now. There has never been any serious doubt about the Slav character of the countryside.

Little now remains of the great Byzantine heritage of Pula. Today its most striking monuments are the ring of fortifications built to defend the bay – Pula was the main naval base of the Austro-Hungarian navy until 1918 – and the Roman amphitheatre. The first is of little interest save to students of recent military architecture; the second is still the outstanding feature of the town, especially if approached by sea. Its enormous bulk – clearly it was far too large for Pula alone and was intended to serve the entire province – still dwarfs the modern buildings around it. No picture of Pula would be recognized without its three-tiered magnificence reflected in the calm waters of the bay.

It is one of the most magnificent Roman amphitheatres still

The Roman amphitheatre at Pula

extant, at least to the eye. For it is an empty shell. By some quirk of architectural design the inner tiers, galleries, and arena seem to have been entirely separated, save for connecting wooden beams whose sockets alone remain, from the outer walls. This has had an unusual, though fortunate, result, since the people of Pula, who used the inner parts of the building extensively as a quarry for their houses, were induced to leave the outer circle of walls intact by a far-sighted and patriotic Venetian senator, Gabriele Emo to whose memory later generations erected a plaque with a grateful inscription that is – or was – embedded in the amphitheatre walls.

The amphitheatre covers about 17,000 square yards, and is estimated to have seated about 21,000 spectators. Even what remains is a remarkable architectural achievement, as the tiers are so arranged as to make maximum use of the natural hillside on which Pula is built.

The beauty of the building and its commanding situation are such that, at the time of Pula's decline, there was a project to remove it stone by stone and re-erect it on a suitable site on the Venetian Lido. Another was to fill the vast interior with earth and stone and convert it into a fortress. Luckily, both were abandoned.

Pula was re-founded, for the site had already been in use for centuries, by Augustus as a veterans' colony under the name of Pietas Juliae, from which the modern name is derived. It rapidly grew rich, largely as a staging point between Ancona and Zadar (Zara) and the Dalmatian cities, and many fragments of Roman magnificence still remain to supplement the appeal of the great amphitheatre.

The appearances of Pietas Juliae in world history have been macabre. It was here that Crispus, the eldest son of Constantine the Great, met in 326 a death as mysterious as the charges laid against him. Only a few years later, in 354, Gallus, the indiscreet brother of Julian the Apostate, was executed either here in Pula or perhaps on the nearby island of Cres.

But we must return to modern times. Just outside the bay of Pula lie the beautiful islands of Brioni, where Marshal Tito has a summer residence. The Brioni Islands were a German headquarters during the last war and were very heavily bombed.

The Marshal displays a close personal interest in Istrian products. At all his receptions at which I was present I noticed that
the wines and vermouth of Poreč were served. Very good they
were, too!

Two more of the Istrian cities – Poreč (Parentium) and Koper
(Aegida – Capodistria) – were also 'colonies', but apparently of
lower rank than Pula. Until A.D. 493 when, with the rest of Istria,
Poreč became for a time part of the Gothic Kingdom its history
is obscure and probably insignificant. It then became the seat of
one of the newly created Istrian bishoprics, and a remarkable man,
Euphrasius, formerly a decurion of the city, was appointed Bishop.
His appointment was confirmed after the conquest of the city by
the Byzantine armies in 539. It was Euphrasius who built the
basilica of Poreč, still the glory of the city, probably on an even
earlier foundation. Though smaller, the basilica has all the
magnificence of the great Byzantine basilicas of Ravenna and
Aquileia. Its mosaics, though damaged by the centuries, are still
impressive. Those composed in the time of Euphrasius have the
pure style and hieratic dignity of the best Byzantine art; a second
group, composed seven centuries later (about 1277), apparently
in the time of another Euphrasius – the names are most confusing
– attempt a more natural style that seems out of keeping with the
medium. It would be extremely interesting to know more of these
mosaics. For the same transformation took place in the frescoes of
the mediaeval Serbian monasteries – most of which were too poor
to afford mosaic. The early Byzantine stiffness and dignity were
replaced by a more vigorous line and greater naturalism which in
many ways antedated the painters of the Italian Renaissance. The
Serbs were far more successful, incidentally, in fresco than in
mosaic. It was, in fact, an early flowering of the creative spirit of
the Slavs, only too soon suppressed by the Turkish invasion. But
of that, more in its place.

The church was reported as destroyed in an invasion of the
Slavs who sacked Poreč in A.D. 961. But they do not seem to have
done as much damage as the chronicler attributed to them – *nuper
a nefandis Sclavis et duris barbaris destructum* – for most of the earlier
architecture and much of the original mosaic escaped their fury.

Perhaps more damage has been done to the basilica by nature

than by the heathen Slavs. The whole western coastline of Istria is gradually sinking, and both here at Poreč and at many other cities of the coast the floor level of the principal churches has twice had to be raised within Christian historical times. Consequently floor has been built upon floor, and a trap-door affords tantalizing glimpses of older, and seemingly better, mosaic pavements, Byzantine underlying Venetian.

Another of the Istrian cities is Piran, on a rocky peninsula near the seaside resort of Portorož. Like Trogir in Dalmatia, it is a museum town, with almost every street and building recalling the tempestuous municipal life of the Middle Ages. Its main square, known as the Ghetto Square, perhaps recalls one of the many immigrations that so often repeopled devastated Istria.

Piran has another link with Trogir. In each town the lion of St. Mark which the Venetians inserted into every public building, whether they built it or not, has closed its book with its pacific inscription. The only difference is that the Piran lions are still in place; that of Trogir has been removed from its place over the main gate of the city and now moulders in a municipal museum.

The Yugoslav government is trying to develop Piran into a resort for artists and writers and a more ideal spot could hardly have been chosen, if in fact ideal surroundings produce great works of art. My own feeling is that artificially fostered communities of this sort rarely produce anything worth having. A Yugoslav artist of my acquaintance told me that those artists who want to live in Istria have mainly gone to Rovinj, a typical Adriatic fishing harbour a few miles south of Piran.

There is little accommodation for visitors at Piran. But that is of no matter, since the town is within a few minutes walk of Portorož, where there is a magnificent hotel. Built in the palmy days of the Dual Monarchy for the Austro-Hungarian nobility, it has a spaciousness denied this more penurious age. Also it has been tactfully and efficiently restored by the Slovene tourist authorities.

Despite the upheavals in the coastal cities, the Slavs of the inland villages slowly developed their own art, quite independently of Venetian influences. Theirs was a hard, peasant life, continually bedevilled by the exactions of constantly changing feudal overlords.

The frescoed churches of Istria are, therefore, small and difficult to find, but they have a charm that makes the effort well worth the while. Perhaps the most beautiful are those at Beram, near Pazin, and at Hrastovlje, not far from Koper. The little churches themselves are Romanesque in style and of uncertain date, but the frescoes were added in the fifteenth and sixteenth centuries. The name of the painter of the Beram church – St. Mary of Škriljine – is known. He was Vincent of Kastav, a little village on the far side of Mt. Učka overlooking the Kvarner Gulf. He painted the frescoes in 1471. Those at Hrastovlje were painted by a certain Johannes, a pupil of the Tyrolean painter Leonhard of Brixen. It is probable that Vincent was also his pupil.

Hrastovlje is a fortress church, surrounded by a massive stone rampart as a defence against Turkish and possibly also pirate raids. The frescoes have a strong Gothic influence but there are also echoes of Byzantine painting, probably from the great basilica at Poreč, and many of the inscriptions are in glagolitic, the first Slav alphabet, of which I shall have more to say later. Possibly Istria was the last place in which it was publicly used, for by the fifteenth century Catholic intolerance had almost suppressed its use in Dalmatia.

The pastel colours, mellowed by age, make these little churches shine like dark jewels, and the peasant simplicity of these interpretations of the Christian legend remind one of the present-day Croatian primitives, men like Generalić and Hegedušić, who paint the daily life of their villages in simple, direct terms and great subtlety of colour. The Dance of Death, a favourite subject of Gothic painters, is to be found both at Beram and Hrastovlje. That at Hrastovlje is twenty-one feet long. It shows the equality of man in face of the gaunt skeleton wielding its scythe. Kings, popes and bishops alike are mown down, but the peasants and labourers are shown in the little church going about their accustomed tasks. Possibly their daily life was enough a dance of death to make any allusion to it unnecessary. Even more moving is the birth of a wide-eyed, full-breasted Eve from Adam's rib and the calm serenity of the Virgin suckling her child.

Beyond Piran is Koper and the frontier, and then Trieste which is not in my bailiwick. Let us return to Rijeka and the Kvarner.

CHAPTER II

The Islands of the Kvarner

Rijeka, Sušak and Trsat – Celestial house-moving – Tunny-ladders – The fishes of the Adriatic – Dalmatian cookery – The damages of war.

Rijeka (or Fiume: the word only means 'river') is the gateway to the Kvarner Gulf; it is also the most convenient centre for boats along the Dalmatian and Istrian coasts. It is not to my mind a very attractive town and, as compared with the other seacoast cities, singularly unlovely. I have always preferred Sušak, on the other side of the river, now almost a suburb of Rijeka. Once, in the early part of the war, when Italy was belligerent and Yugoslavia still neutral, Allied planes were deceived by the lights of Sušak and dumped their bombs there. But between the wars Sušak was a city in its own right and the river was the frontier, where sober Yugoslav gendarmes faced gaily dressed carabinieri across a few feet of iron bridge. It used to be a striking example in economic geography to watch the busy though cramped harbour of Sušak while only a few yards away were the lonely quays and almost deserted harbour of Fiume, as it was then, a mere frontier port without an adequate hinterland. It was the condottiere exploits of d'Annunzio that forced the Yugoslavs to hand Fiume over to the Italians despite the terms of the peace treaty.

But there are some interesting places nearby. Trsat, for example. In the days when Sušak was a mere suburb, Trsat was a fortress and a little group of houses around the old Frankopan church. Even now the atmosphere of the two places is entirely different. At the foot of the long stairway of 412 steps which leads from the main square of Sušak to the Frankopan church everything is busy and energetic; at the top of the stairway all is quiet and peaceful.

Pliny mentions Trsat as a Liburnian town, which later became the Roman Tersatica, but in Roman times it did not occupy the

B 33

site where it now stands. Probably Roman Tersatica is buried somewhere beneath modern Rijeka. It was taken by the Croats in their forays of the sixth century and later, in 799, by the Franks, who ruled a short-lived empire that stretched almost to Belgrade.

But it was in May 1291 that the miracle occurred that made Trsat famous. Visitors may interpret it according to their degree of faith or credulity. It was then that the angels brought from Nazareth to Trsat the House of the Virgin, performing this feat of house-moving in a single night and placing the Holy House on the site of the present Frankopan church. Apparently the people of Trsat were considered unworthy of so great a miracle for in February 1294 the angelic messengers again removed the holy building, this time to Recanati in Italy where it is still famous as the shrine of Loreto. But Trsat has always remained a place of pious pilgrimage.

From the so-called Roman tower of the Frankopan castle one can look out far over the Kvarner with its astonishing patchwork of colour on sea and land. The winds of the Kvarner are fickle and capricious, coming and going without apparent reason, and under their gentle pressure the sea towards evening turns to the most extravagant colours: cobalt, ultramarine, deep reddish-purple, green and the wonderful deep Adria blue.

Not that the Kvarner is always so mild. In winter the winds are terrible, and the offerings of sailors who have escaped their fury almost fill the Church of Our Lady of Trsat, which was built by the Frankopans on the site of the vanished House of the Virgin.

On a slab in the main aisle is an inscription stating that beneath lies the head of that most famous knight of Klis, Petar Kružić, the Uskok leader. But I found no one to tell me of its historical associations, so I looked mostly at the many pictures of sailing-ships battling with the waves, and read the pious vows of those who survived.

Amongst these appears, somewhat incongruously, a double-page newspaper illustration of the sinking of the *Titanic* in 1912.

In almost every little cove of the Kvarner you will see the tunny-ladders pointing to the skies like warning fingers. On a clear day, or even more on a clear starlit night, the fishermen sit there unmoving, watching the surface of the waters. Usually these ladders are at the entrance to narrow coves where the tunny come in to feed. From his high perch, 20 or 30 feet above the water, the watcher can see far down into the depths and pick out, by day, the dark forms of the shoal or, by night, the light glinting on their scales. The fishermen are organized in small bands, each taking his two-hours' watch on the ladder. When the shoal is well within the bay, they close the entrance with nets and gradually round up the mass of giant fish. For the tunny grows to a very large size and its steak-like flesh preserved in oil is a delicacy. A good catch may prove the fortune of a group of fishermen and there are rejoicings when it is brought to port in one of the small fishing villages.

The actual scene of the catch, with its mounting excitement as the great silvery bodies of the monstrous fish are landed, is intensely dramatic and has been used effectively in several films.

The tunny-ladders, however, seem to be typical of the Kvarner and the Croatian coast, and I have never seen them south of Rab, or in Greece, despite the many references to the tunny in classical literature.

The eastern coast of the Adriatic, with its rocky bays and innumerable islands, has always provided better fishing grounds than the low, sandy Italian shore, and the competition for the best fishing has gone on between Yugoslav and Italian fishermen for centuries. The Yugoslavs, having the right of possession, get the best of it.

Fishing among these islands, especially the outer ring, is very good indeed, and the islands are seldom visited for any other purpose. Most of the cities and watering-places with attractions for the tourist and the student are – Vis excepted – in the inner ring. Lack of drinking-water makes them unsuitable for tourists, and the inhabitants either get their water by boat from some more favoured spot or rely on the uncertain aid of rainwater catchments, only too apt to fail them in the long rainless summers. I have visited several of these islands and have had a most enjoyable time at the cost of a little discomfort.

Since the war a fresh initiative of Yugoslav tourism has made them more accessible. Several times during the summer, motor caïques leave Rijeka for the outer islands on a trip designed especially for the fisherman. A little brochure written in an English as remarkable as the trip itself gives all the details. The boat goes from Rijeka to Lošinj and Silba, still within the pale of civilization, and then makes for the outer islands, whose names sound like a roll of drums: Molat, Dugi Otok, Veli Rat, Sali, Kornat, Sila, Mrtvac (the corpse), Mana, Jadra, Lavsa. Incidentally, there can be no better place in the world for the post-war sport of underwater fishing.

Travellers may stay in the caïques or take tents with them. On their way they will pass one of the natural curiosities of the Kvarner Gulf, the island of Susak (not Sušak – mind your diacritics!). In contrast to the other Yugoslav islands, Susak (the dried-up one) is a sandbank created by under-water springs some 40 fathoms down in the sea itself.

These are the fishermen's islands; and their catch is a rich one. The Adriatic is teeming with hundreds of varieties of fish, many of them affording excellent sport and almost all of them excellent to eat. I admit that my own knowledge of them is more from the viewpoint of the gourmet than the sportsman, but no matter.

In the Kvarner itself there is of course the tunny; excellent in oil as an hors-d'oeuvre, but even better fresh as a grilled fish-steak, as firm and satisfying as the best beefsteak. Then there are the scampi, or Adriatic prawns, equally good *au naturel* or fried in a light batter. Also little soft-shelled crabs in season, which you can eat whole, and, of course, excellent oysters. A really skilful cook will usually manage to get from the local fishermen more exotic crustaceans, prstići, or 'little fingers', rather like razor-shells, datule, and other fruits of the sea. Then there are always first-class lobsters and salt-water crawfish, as well as the fearsome-looking Adriatic crab, which is bright pink with long spidery legs like a child's drawing.

As regards the real fishes, their name is legion. Nearly all of them are best fried in oil. But here I must sound a note of warning to the eager gourmet. The Dalmatian oil is first-class, but it is unrefined and the smell of the pressed olives still clings around it. Like Greek resinated wine, when you get a taste for it, you prefer it to its more refined relations. But if you have not, then ask for your fish to be cooked in 'French' oil.

The Dalmatians are not master cooks. They have none of the subtleties. But they can choose and grill a fish to perfection. Grilled tunny I have mentioned above, but suggest it be eaten to the accompaniment of a glass of rakija, the local spirit, of which more hereafter. The zubatac (dentale), well named 'toothy', is firm fleshed and considered a great delicacy, though I myself prefer the cipol, which the Dalmatians unfairly neglect. The orad, with a head too big for its body, is also best grilled, while the molo is perhaps the only Adriatic fish that is better boiled or steamed. Avoid the morena; it is a mouthful of bones. But the little gaily coloured barbuni, well known from accounts of Lucullus' banquets, make very delicate eating. A good cook will not grill these too much, or they may become dry. Less delicate, but excellent for a quick light meal, are grilled fresh sardines. We are so used to seeing the sardine come, cooked and headless, out of a tin that I have known English visitors deny that they are the same fish. They are. And they are also excellent salted, as an hors-d'oeuvre.

It is always well, and as a rule not too difficult, to get on good terms with the local cook. He is usually proud of his art and not too reticent about its secrets. For the question of eating and drinking is very important. I shall return to it later on, not only for Dalmatia but for other districts of Yugoslavia as well, for each region has its own delicacies and its own cuisine. For one thing, there is much truth in the saying: tell me what you eat and I will tell you what you are. Another and most practical reason is that a disordered tummy is a most irritating travelling companion. It is even more irritating when it is not necessary. Therefore beginners in Dalmatia must beware of the oil.

Bakalar, a common dish in smaller Dalmatian hotels, is merely imported dried cod. It is best avoided, for only the Italian cooks of Vicenza can make it a tasty dish.

I am, of course, assuming that the intelligent traveller prefers to eat in the local restaurants. The cuisine in the big, modern hotels is only too often apt to be 'international', which usually means poor French and is most uninteresting. With a few noble exceptions it is harmless, but dull. This is one of the curses of organized tourism and is often unavoidable. The brave man who strikes out for himself will be amply rewarded.

Incidentally, by far the best cuisine in Yugoslavia is the Serbian. I would even go so far as to say it is the best in Europe. There is a post-war saying that to be a perfect Yugoslav one should 'eat like a Serb, dress like a Croat, have a salary like a Slovene and work like a Montenegrin'.

The main fury of the partisan wars was in Bosnia and the Lika, where widespread damage took place. Many villages were completely destroyed and many others retain only a few fragments of their former picturesqueness having been rebuilt in practical but not very beautiful form. Apart from the fact that these areas were the scene of the fiercest fighting, the local building material, at least in Bosnia, is wood. In Dalmatia the fighting was less severe and the local building material is stone. None the less, air bombardments and commando raids took their toll.

Zadar, or Zara as it was then called, was an Italian enclave in Slav Dalmatia and suffered more than fifty air-raids. The famous ninth-century Croat church of St. Donat however escaped very serious injury and has been repaired with the original stones. Korčula also was seriously damaged. A photo taken shortly after the war shows it as a city of empty-shell houses, and in the middle forties one was advised not to visit it. Some smaller places, such as Makarska and Vela Luka, also suffered severely. But the ravages have been repaired and the visitor is not likely to notice them, save for the crop of war memorials and commemorative plaques which recall, with justifiable pride, the exploits of the partisan armies. Such memorials are apt to be dull for those who have no personal interest in them and after the memory of those they commemorate has faded, but their frequency is less to be deplored in that the Dalmatians and the men of the mountain ranges along the sea-coast have a grand tradition of sculpture that has produced such giants as Ivan Meštrović and Toma Rosandić.

There are three ways from Rijeka southwards. One is by the deep-water channel – the Vela Vrata or Great Gate, between Cres and the Istrian mainland – the second by the Mala Vrata or Little Gate between Cres and Krk, and the third by a narrow channel along the Croatian coast itself. The small coasting steamers take the third route, which is the most interesting.

The twin island of Cres-Lošinj can easily be seen from Rijeka harbour. Up to the last war it was Italian, though the inhabitants were mainly Slav. Perhaps owing to this political isolation from their fellows, they and some of the Istrians have preserved two of the least-known Croat dialects, the so-called 'ća' and 'ča' dialects, that being the local way of saying 'What?' The mainland Croats mostly say 'Kaj' and the Serbs 'Što', and the dialects are named accordingly.

It is one of the best-wooded islands, mainly with stone-pines which seem to thrive on the karst and, where present, preserve a certain amount of soil on which other growths can live. The two main towns, Mali (little) and Veliki (great) Lošinj, are only a few minutes apart, but with their harbours facing in different directions, being on opposite sides of the long, narrow island. In Austro-Hungarian days they were one of the favourite seaside resorts of the Austrian empresses and their court ladies. Being near the open sea the winds are more constant and reliable, so that Lošinj, whether Small or Great, is a wonderful centre for sailing and fishing among the smaller islands: Unije, Sv. Petar, the curious Susak, Silba, Olib, Premuda, &c. In addition to fish, these smaller islands produce an excellent local cheese.

The northern part of the twin-island, Cres, with the little town of the same name, has all the charm of a land apparently almost untouched by the passing of time. Its pine-woods are the home of a special kind of polecat, the skins of which, according to the Abbé Fortis, were carefully collected and sent to Venice, where local artisans had the art of dressing them to resemble martens. The feudal tribute of the island in the early Middle Ages to the Most Serene Republic was *pelles marturinas numero quadraginta*, to be paid on Christmas Day.

Curious relics of otherwise rare or rapidly disappearing fauna are to be found on several of the islands. Korčula is probably the last home of the European jackal, while Mljet (Meleda) used to have a plague of mongooses; but these were the descendants of a recent importation intended to rid the island of snakes, a job in which I am assured they succeeded.

CHAPTER III

Krk – Isle of the Frankopans

*'Beware the hands of Senj' – Krk, island of the Frankopans – Dalmatian
wines and rakijas – Glagolitic letters.*

I decided to visit the island of Krk and took the easternmost
channel between the Velebit mountains and the high, rocky
shores of the island. The ship passes by Bakar, to stop at Kraljevica,
Crikvenica, Novi Vinodol, Selce and Senj, all of them important
places in the history of Croatia and all connected with the rule
of the Zrinjski and Frankopan families, who so long held the
lordship in these waters.

At Kraljevica the whole town is in the shadow of the Zrinjski
castle, while at Novi Vinodol the companion castle of the Frankopans is scarcely less impressive. Here in 1266 was signed the
famous Statute of Vinodol, a most remarkable document for its
time, which for many years served as a charter of liberty for the
semi-independent district of the Wine Valley, which stretched up
into Istria.

Crikvenica, on the other hand, though tracing its origin to a
Greek colony, has an air of modernity, given it by a number of
large modern hotels. Indeed, it is one of the most fashionable
places on the whole coast.

Senj, however, is far the most interesting of these little places.
It is famous both for its stormy weather and its stormy history.
There is nearly always a slight swell in the open roadstead, even
on the calmest days, while directly opposite, between the islands
of Krk and Prvić, is the notorious Gate or Senjska Vrata. Many
of the spirited drawings in the Trsat church commemorate successful navigation of these troublous waters.

In the later Middle Ages Senj was a walled city with jurisdiction
over all the smaller towns of the Croatian littoral and its inhabitants, at the height of their power, extended their frontiers to Istria

and as far south as Obrovac. It was the home of the Uskoks, desperate refugees from the Neretva valley, who refused to surrender to the Turks and made a last stand for freedom in rocky Senj. And very successful they were. For many years Senj was an independent state, even having its own emissaries in the western courts of Europe, especially Spain. Their main duty was to encourage the rivalry between the Empire and the Venetians, by which they lived, and their methods were bribery and intrigue. For a time they had been the Venetians' allies, but when, in a desperate attempt to recover from the Turks their earlier stronghold of Klis, the Venetians turned against them and supported the Turks, the Uskoks regarded Venice as their deadliest enemy. Their courage and ferocity became proverbial in that city: *Iddio vi guardi dalle mani de Segnani.*

The fame of their great leader, Ivo of Senj, was not restricted to his city. He fought at Lepanto in 1571, in Cyprus, in Egypt and in the Morea, and at the battle of the Kupa in Bosnia in 1593 is said to have performed the almost incredible feat of routing 50,000 Turks with only 800 of his ferocious Uskoks!

His exploits have doubtless been exaggerated by the popular poets, the odds growing greater with every generation. But undoubtedly he was a mighty warrior, and the story of his death is one of the most beautiful of the Yugoslav heroic ballads:

> *A dream has dreamt the mother of Ivo,*
> *Darkness she saw fall upon Senj,*
> *The clear heavens burst asunder,*
> *The shimmering moon fell down to earth,*
> *On the church of St. Rose in the midst of Senj.*
>
> *And the stars were swept across the sky,*
> *And the dawn rose up all red with blood,*
> *And the cuckoo bird she heard a-calling,*
> *In the midst of Senj, on Senj's white church.*
>
> *When from her dream the dame awakened,*
> *Her staff she took in her right hand,*
> *And went forthwith to St. Rose's church;*

And there she told the Archpriest Nedeljko,
Told him all that she had dreamed.
And when the old man had heard her out,
'Twas thus he did expound the dream:

Hear me, O hear me, aged mother!
'Twas an evil dream, and worse shall befall.
That darkness fell on the town of Senj,
It is that desolate it shall remain;
That the clear heavens burst asunder
And the shimmering moon fell down to earth,
It is that Ivo is to die.

That the stars were swept across the sky,
It is that many a widow shall be;
That the dawn rose up all red with blood,
It is that thou shalt be left to weep;
That the cuckoo bird by St. Rose sang,
It is that the Turks shall plunder it,
And me in my old age they shall slay.

(Translation – Prof. Seton-Watson)

The huge machicolated castle brooding over the harbour is the famous Nehaj (Fear-not).

At the height of the Uskoks' power the fighting men of Senj were not numerous; a generous estimate would put them at 2,000. But they drew to their standard all sorts of desperate men escaping from Turkish or Venetian misrule, who were known as *venturieri*, a name one is tempted to translate as 'brethren of the coast'. Travellers in the eighteenth century mention a number of Englishmen among them.

But their ferocity, their daring and above all their consummate seamanship made them dangerous enemies. Light craft they easily defeated, while an armada of the cumbrous Venetian war-galleys did not dare to trust itself to the stormy waters of the Senjska Vrata. For a long time the Uskoks defied the Venetians by sea and kept the forces of the Empire at bay on land by making full use of the inaccessibility of their stronghold and, if rumour does not lie, by a judicious distribution of their spoils among the courtiers and ladies of the Imperial Court. Be that as it may, attempts to suppress them were half-hearted and ineffectual, though the history of their wars and shifting alliances is filled with incidents when both sides used the most hideous cruelty. It was not until the early seventeenth century that the imperial forces transported the Uskoks inland, burned their ships and broke the power of Senj. Uskok names from this transplantation may still be found in the former Military Frontiers, in Istria and elsewhere.

The name Uskok, by the way, is neither territorial nor tribal; it merely means 'one who leaps over'. A good translation would be 'reiver'.

An interesting point for the visitor to note at Senj is the absence of the typical small columns frequently found cut in relief at the corners of important houses in the other Dalmatian cities. Such columns were an indication of nobility. Senj, however, had no privileged caste; it was a rough-and-ready democracy.

Abbé Fortis, writing in 1787, describes Senj as a small backward port whose inhabitants, while still maintaining a certain independence, courtesy, and nobility of spirit, were much oppressed by the bureaucratic tyranny of the Military Government of the Lika.

Old Fortis is a good guide, with a sarcastic turn of phrase that is very readable. He saw Dalmatia at its worst, and does not hesitate to lay about him manfully, whether at Venetian neglect, Austrian militarism or local sloth. Although a priest, he does not spare his own order when, as so often at that time, it was idle and vicious. Although an Italian, he has a good understanding of, and sympathy with, the Croats or 'Morlacchi', as he calls them. He is a first-class observer of all forms of natural history, a practical man who would today be called an economist and a fine antiquarian. But he does not suffer fools gladly. 'For those who are ignorant or know little of this science (natural history) are commonly the most severe and illiberal in their accusations.' Alas, that is only too true of himself when he deals with Slav etymologies, where he makes some most startling howlers!

But we have stopped too long at Senj. Through the formidable Senjska Vrata the boat turns to Baška on Krk. This island is full of violent contrasts, a sort of Dalmatia in miniature. On the side facing the Velebit it is rough and craggy, with a fringe of forest rare in Dalmatia. On this shore is Vrbnik, the subject of one of the loveliest Dalmatian folk-songs. On the western side it is terraced karst, sloping down to beautiful beaches and sheltered bays.

It, too, has a distinct character of its own, different from that of the other islands. Perhaps this is due to its history; for 400 years it was the principal seat of the Frankopans, who were probably local Slav nobles by origin. The derivation from the ancient patrician family of Frangipani, one of the last of the senatorial families, the gens Anicius, was probably due to a typical piece of mediaeval flattery on the part of Pope Martin V, whom Nikola Frankopan visited in Rome in 1426. The wily Pope wished to have the support of such powerful princes and led them to believe that they were of ancient Roman origin. Mediaeval genealogists were fond of tracing the origin of all sorts of unlikely people to the gens Anicius, including Gregory the Great, St. Thomas Aquinas and Francis of Assisi. The adoption by the Frankopans of the ancient Frangipani arms – two golden lions breaking bread, a memory of the great flood in Rome of 717 – dates only from the fifteenth century. Before that time the princes of Krk used the coat-of-arms of the island: gold stars on a white ground. The first Venetian governor of the island, Antonio Vinciguerra (1480), who was incidentally its first historian, says that they were of Slav origin and, though he was no friend of the Frankopans, there is no reason to suppose he deliberately lied. Fortis repeats some of his bad opinions. Perhaps the name is from Franko Ban, which is a Slav title borrowed from the Avars.

Like all mediaeval nobles, they were a turbulent brood. The island of Krk and all the cities of the nearby mainland are full of their fortresses, their churches and their monastery bequests. But, despite Vinciguerra, they managed to make themselves beloved of their people, and the national costume of Krk, now rarely seen, a melancholy affair of heavy black cloth, is said to have been adopted in memory of the last of the princes of Krk, who was, at least in popular story, cheated of his inheritance by the Venetians.

I had heard the story often enough, but was indeed lucky when on Krk to get the words of a folk-song still sung at that time and which commemorates, accurately enough, the Venetian treachery. I give it in a free translation, only regretting that I cannot reproduce the characteristic dialect of the island:

> *When the pale Venetians*
> *With armament of galleys*
> *Set sail to Omišalj,*
> *Came ashore a party*
> *To invite Prince Ivan*
> *To a great rejoicing.*
>
> *When all were together*
> *Drinking the red wine,*
> *They bore away our Ivan*
> *To the Cresko More.*
>
> *Then the Prince, our Ivan,*
> *Bitterly regarded*
> *How the false Venetian*
> *Had faithlessly deceived him:*
>
> *'O my lovely towers,*
> *Lovely and spacious,*
> *How beautifully I built you!*
> *And now I cannot*
> *Come once more to you.*
>
> *'To whom shall I leave you?*
> *To the skimming swallows*
> *That on summer evenings*
> *Fly above thy towers.*
> *To me a sad memorial*
> *And to the world accusing*
> *The treachery of Venice.'*

Under the Frankopans the people of Krk were free peasant farmers, and under Venetian rule they were not serfs. One notices, even today, amongst them a freer and more independent manner than amongst the people of neighbouring Rab, who had a tradition of serfdom until the liberation of 1918.

Much of Yugoslavia is vineyard country, and Dalmatia most of all. Before the war the Dalmatian wines were little known in England, at least in their pure form, for large quantities used to be sent to Cette and other unscrupulous ports to make up the cheaper export wines of France. Since the war, Yugoslav wines have been gaining ground on the English market, though, as a matter of fact, few of these come from Dalmatia. A probable reason is that most of the grapes are either home-grown or pro-duced in very small co-operatives, which makes it difficult to maintain an absolutely even standard of bottling. Also there is strenuous competition from the larger Serbian and, strange to say, Macedonian wine co-operatives, which import their wines into England through the firm of R. & W. Teltscher. Fifteen years ago, to speak of Macedonian wines was rather like talking about Alaskan pineapples; they were non-existent. But today the wine co-operatives at Kavadarci and elsewhere make excellent low-cost wines greatly appreciated in England and which, in my opinion, taste better than the more familiar Slovene wines.

But in Dalmatia the gourmet's deprival is the visitor's advantage. The Dalmatian wines blend perfectly with the local food and are delicious in the long, cool evenings when, after a day's bathing, fishing or sailing, you take a seat outside the local kafana and watch the life of the townspeople, who never seem to go to bed. Now and again, though more rarely nowadays, you may hear groups singing the lovely Dalmatian folk-songs, which are still really songs of the folk and have not yet quite descended to the demi-monde of the *café chantant*.

Most of the better known wines are sold in bottles, especially when imported from other districts or sold in the more fashionable resorts. But in the small kafanas wine is sold in bulk in the carafe. This is the real wine-lover's opportunity. He is not forced to finish a bottle just because it has been opened, but can taste and choose until he has found one to his taste. In most cases the landlord is pleased and flattered to find the visitor taking an intelligent interest in the local wine, and will offer suggestions that are not to be despised.

Unless you get an unscrupulous innkeeper – and there are such in all countries – Yugoslav wine is pure. There are no fortified wines on sale. Wines are classed as belo (white), crno (black, which we should call red) and ružica (rosé).

I realize, however, that the average visitor does not remain in any one place long enough to become a connoisseur of the local vintages. As a rule, he must depend on the advice of his host and the name on the bottle. Therefore I will mention a few of the better known wines to be found in Dalmatia. Most of them are local, though one or two favourite varieties may have been brought to the coast from inland vineyards.

One of the best – and commonest – wines in the islands is Black Vis (Viško Crno), from the island of the same name. It is a heavy red wine, rather like a good Chianti, and is excellent with meat dishes or with heavy, meaty fish like tunny. From the same island comes the golden-yellow Vugava, fourteen degrees in strength, and a somewhat aromatic wine of an amber colour known as Grk (the Greek), from its resemblance to the wines of that country. If you are lucky, you may find a bottle of the wine of Biševo, a tiny island off Vis which still preserves the original European vine, having escaped the almost universal plague of the phylloxera.

From the vineyards of the Riviera of the Seven Castles near Split comes Opol, a lighter red wine rather like a claret, while the slightly heavier Dingač comes from the peninsula of Pelješac. From Hercegovina come two excellent wines: Blatina (red) and Zilavka (white), which are often served on the coast, especially around Dubrovnik. An excellent Burgundy-type wine from Negotin in Serbia, Prokupac, is also frequently to be found. The light white wines of Istria are served at Marshal Tito's receptions. An excellent red wine, of individual flavour, is Teran from the vineyards of the karst above Opatija.

But these few names, which could be multiplied almost indefinitely, should not prevent the enthusiastic gourmet from making his own tests of the local vintages.

Everyone who has been in Yugoslavia comes back with a taste for rakija. Rakija merely means spirit, and has no connexion, except philologically, with arrack or the rakis of Greece and

Turkey. The favourite rakija is distilled from plums (šljivovica) and is mainly made in Serbia, Bosnia, or Slavonia, but can be obtained anywhere in the country. It is a taste that grows on one; but beginners must remember that it is very volatile and very strong. Šljivovica is distilled by the state as well as by the peasants themselves, whose product is apt to vary greatly. A local Dalmatian rakija is distilled from mountain herbs and is called travarica – from trava, 'grass'. It is excellent. A yellowish, pungent rakija – klekovača – is distilled from juniper, but has no flavour of Western gin. Grape rakijas include komovica and lozovača, the latter rather coarser in taste. These wine rakijas should never be confused with brandy. Their taste is entirely different. Pelinkovac, distilled from wormwood, is medicinal only – its taste is horrible and very bitter, but it is said to be good for the liver or for a hangover. I do not recommend it.

The best and most usual way of drinking these rakijas is with light snacks before a meal – the excellent Dalmatian ham, pršut (a kind of dried smoked meat cut very thin), various salted and smoked fish, anchovies, peppers in oil, and a host of other delicacies. A point to be remembered is that these are served free with the drinks in most Balkan and Near Eastern countries – in Yugoslavia they are purchased separately.

After dinner, coffee, sweet dessert wines, or liqueurs. Coffee tastes best and is best here in the Turkish manner; but of course you must say before it is made whether you want it sweet or not. For, once made, it cannot be stirred, or the results will be incredibly nasty. My own experience, over many years in the Balkans and the Near East, is that the Bosnians make the best Turkish coffee, better even than the Turks themselves.

Of the sweet wines, prošek (from the Italian prosecco) is a heavy wine of the malaga type. When dark, it is excellent; when light, it is apt to be wishy-washy. A good, sweet dessert wine from Istria, to be found mainly in the north of Dalmatia, is refosco. A single glass is usually enough.

Yugoslavia has one excellent liqueur, the extra dry kirsch of Zadar. But the number of sweet rakijas is legion. One of the best is made from black cherries (višnjevača); another good one, but hard to find, is made from green walnuts (orahovača).

The pear rakija tastes, probably unjustifiably, of chemicals.

One evening I walked around Baška. It is a charming little place, though newer than most Dalmatian towns. The earliest inscription that I found dated only to 1525.

When I want to find out about a Dalmatian town, I ask for the local archaeologist, even as in an inland town the best person to talk to is the doctor. There is nearly always one such person, in even the smallest places, who takes an intelligent interest in the past and, generally speaking, they are far from being dry-as-dust bookworms. They are usually, on the other hand, energetic and enterprising, as their hobby takes them far afield among the villages and to long-deserted sites on coast or mountain-side. Even those who might have become bookworms by temperament have usually to ransack the libraries of monasteries so distant that they have escaped pirate raids or more civilized pillage in order to find the books they want.

This time I approached the subject by asking if there were anyone in the town who could read the old glagolitic books, and was at once sent to the parish priest, Dom Vinko Premuda.

I could see he was rather intrigued at discovering an Englishman who knew anything about glagolitic, and he dug out for me manuscripts that he had found in out-of-the-way monastic libraries where they had long remained unregarded.

For glagolitic is the step-sister of the Roman Church. The first Slavonic apostles, Cyril and Methodius, lived before the Great Schism and were in touch with Rome as well as Constantinople. The Slavonic alphabet which Cyril invented and used for their church books was not, as many believe, the Cyrillic. That was devised later at Ohrid by their disciples, Kliment and Naum, and named after their master. He used the glagolitic characters. But the new Cyrillic was so much more practical and readable that glagolitic was scarcely known to the eastern Slavs, who after the Schism looked to Constantinople. On the other hand, the Croats, who looked to Rome, never used the Cyrillic, and the glagolitic lettering became more or less synonymous with the Croat Church.

CHAPTER IV

Rab, Zrmanja, Zadar

Background to Rab – Before the Venetians – The mountain channel – Fjord of the Giants – Slav gods and saints – Overland by ship – Yugoslav national costumes – Episode at Bijelo Polje – Zadar.

The boat from Baška to Rab leaves early in the morning. But in summer in Dalmatia the mornings are delightful. It is a pleasure rather than a hardship to get up early. If one is lucky enough to catch the sunrise, one is amply rewarded.

The first sight of Rab is charming. After the rocky wildness of the coast, its grey-green forests of stone-pines seem to welcome one. But these forests have also their sinister secrets. During the last war the Italians had a large concentration camp here, where more than 5,000 Yugoslavs lost their lives.

The boat stops for a moment at Lopar, one of the most pleasing of the smaller resorts. It was the brithplace of the hermit Marinus, who later founded the tiny republic of San Marino in Italy, which is still independent, though known to few save stamp-collectors.

After a succession of beautiful wooded bays, one comes in sight of Rab itself, which is one of the most beautiful cities of Dalmatia. It is a tiny walled stronghold of the Middle Ages, with typical churches and palaces, but has been given a special faery quality of its own by its four graceful campaniles and the massive spiky agaves along the sea-wall and the green forests behind. It is so romantic in appearance that it has almost an air of unreality.

We threaded into the harbour through a series of breakwaters, which seem unnecessarily elaborate in high summer, but are needed in winter to break the force of the wind. The quay was gay and crowded with visitors. The whole atmosphere of Rab is one of gaiety. After Dubrovnik, it is the most fashionable of the Dalmatian resorts. The squadrons of tiny white-sailed pleasure-boats along the quay, like a flock of gulls with outspread wings, add to the charm of the first impression, and the long line of hotels does not spoil the mediaeval character of the city. They are lined up along the quay like willing and discreet servants of the old aristocrat behind them.

I do not like mondaine resorts. But Rab is an exception. For one thing, two minutes on foot or by boat takes one immediately out of the mondaine atmosphere, whither one may return again at night for as much wine, women and song as one desires. The long quay is gay and crowded till late into the night with the most striking fashions that one could desire; not all of them, either, are worn by the visitors. It is wonderful how smart and pleasing the Yugoslav girls manage to look, despite the long years of shortages that the country has been through. There is always a sound of music, and almost everywhere there is dancing. But round the corner of the Princes' Palace, or on the little square near the cathedral, one is back again in the quiet austerity of the Middle Ages. The contrast is striking and exhilarating, like an *omelette surprise*.

Rab is quite small. In half an hour or so one can see all the principal sights. But almost any of the churches and monasteries, of which there are an incredible number for so small a place, have treasures of art and history that repay a much longer study. Few people give them that attention, for the atmosphere of Rab is one of holiday and not of history, although the history is always there like an impalpable essence. No modern city would seem quite so gay without this contrast.

In the cathedral is the head of St Catherine, the patron of the island. An early bishop of Rab was rash enough to doubt the authenticity of this relic and refused to allow it to be carried in procession, which so enraged the people of the town that they threatened to throw him into the sea from the square in front of the cathedral. The fall is considerable. So the head was carried in procession and the bishop obtained a transfer to Italy. The still more miraculous heads of the Three Hebrew Children, Shadrach, Meshach and Abednego, mentioned by Fortis, were apparently too miraculous for later ages to swallow and are no longer to be seen.

The local wine of Rab is excellent. Also, perhaps the best Dalmatian prošek comes from the island. Visitors to Rab often drink it as a table wine, with disastrous results, as its strength is concealed by its sweetness.

It is customary to regard Rab as a Venetian city, and certainly some of the finest buildings date from the Venetian occupation. But the general aspect of the town was already formed before their time. An old picture of the city in the monastery of Sv. Antun, with the Virgin and Christ looking down at it benevolently from cotton-wool clouds of glory, shows it very much as it is today. The long quay with its row of hotels is new and a fourth campanile has been added since that time, but the other changes are insignificant. Rab was once an Illyrian stronghold, the centre of the Ardeian tribe of the Liburnians, whose swift galleys later caused so much trouble to the Romans. It was also a Greek settlement under the name of Neoparis, later a Roman city, then in turn Gothic, Byzantine and Croat, under whose kings it had a local autonomy. The head of St Christopher, according to legend, saved it from a Norman conquest in 1075. It had its own bishopric from 530 to 1823 and its own statutes from Croat times until the

Rab

Venetian conquest. The cathedral church was commenced in the twelfth century, and its campanile is first mentioned in 1212. The Lion of St Mark, here as in many other places in Dalmatia, merely reaped where others had sown.

One of the most colourful characters in Rab's history was the heretic bishop of Rab, de Dominis, who meditated upon the laws of optics and gravitation while at Mass, in many ways forestalling the discoveries of Newton, questioned the power and integrity of the Roman Church, and fled to King James, who gave him an English living, where he wrote a book against Rome; but he at last recanted and was received again into the bosom of Mother Church, only to have his uneasy body exhumed and publicly burnt on the Campo Santo. The family still exists in Yugoslavia and America.

I gazed indifferently upon the supposed Titian in the church of Sv. Andrija. Titians also exist at Osor, Dubrovnik and other places in Dalmatia. Indeed, it would be a fascinating occupation for one with time on his hands to trace the wanderings of this artist, or at least of his works. As some of his Dalmatian paintings are frescoed ceilings he must have spent some time in these parts. The famous Vivarini polyptych in the cathedral is, alas, only a copy. The original was bought by a rich American in 1876 and taken to Boston. The ancient shields, the wonderful carved portals of the Bakota and Marčić-Galzigna families, the graceful campaniles and the grey old bastions faded and blurred into an impression of white sails, sunlight and smiling faces.

It is as well here to point out one complication in reading the history of Dalmatia in Venetian times. Almost all the old families of the coast, most of whom, save at Dubrovnik, still exist, had double names, one Slav, one Italian. When one is merely an adaptation of the other, this is fairly easy to spot. But sometimes they are translations and, unless one knows both languages, this is not so easy. To quote only a few: Gozze-Gučetić, Gondola-Gundulić, Cortenazzi-Jablanović, and so on.

The trip to Obrovac is one of the most magnificent in all Dalmatia. But few visitors know it, and even the average Yugoslav shakes his head and murmurs vaguely about a lake and a canyon. Few have ever been there.

The boat passes Crikvenica and Senj and then heads for the Mountain Channel along the coast of the mainland. Jablanac, described by Fortis as 'a miserable hamlet', is now a pleasant little seaside resort, making a gay patch of colour against the massive grey stone of the Velebit. Its harbour is also in a fine rocky fjord and is a favourite excursion from Rab, but compared with the Zrmanja canyon to Obrovac it is a second-rate affair.

It is from the districts around Jablanac that the Bunjevci come; or at least that is the most probable of the many suggestions for their origin and eighteenth-century writers take it for granted. These Bunjevci now form a curious little racial and religious pocket far up on the northern plain, around Subotica, on the Hungarian border. A digression on their history would take us too far from Dalmatia.

For the next hour or so the journey is impressive but mono-tonous. Maybe this is one of the reasons why it is not popular with tourists. The ship slowly steams down the long channel, with the stony slopes of the Velebit on the one side and the low, rather featureless, shores of Pag on the other. Sometimes the monotony is varied by a short halt at one or another of the villages which perch precariously on the very narrow shelf between the Velebit and the sea. It looks as if a push would send them all sliding into the water, and one wonders how people live in that treeless, vineless and waterless solitude. It was only recently that the coast road from Rijeka to Ulcinj was completed, which gives them some communication with the outer world. The boats call regularly, but infrequently.

Generally speaking, it is best to see Dalmatia by ship, so that one can visit the islands and peer into the fjords. But just here it is far better by car. The view from the road over the sea is magnificent; that from the sea over the mountains impressive, but monotonous.

There are many dolphins in the canal, and their graceful antics enliven the journey. The old classical superstition that the dolphin is the friend of man still lives in these waters and no Dalmation fisherman will harm one.

Behind these frowning mountains lies the Lika. Many of them descendants of the Uskoks, the Ličani are among the toughest of the Yugoslavs, and their villages are to be found in the most desolate regions of the karst. Some of the fiercest fighting in the partisan wars took place in this area.

On the right is the long, low island of Pag. The capital city, Pag itself, is on a salt lagoon with a narrow entrance towards the main channel. I have never had a chance to go there. But, by all accounts, it must be an interesting little place. It was both a Liburnian and a Roman city, though in each case the site is outside the mediaeval town. Both were doubtless established because of the richness of the salt-pans, for there is little else to recommend the site and navigation is both difficult and dangerous. The town has a fine fifteenth-century cathedral, which escaped even the detailed researches of T. G. Jackson, and is famous for its lace-workers.

The main hill of the island Pag is named after St Vid, and indeed in the purely Slavonic districts, by which I mean those in which the Venetian clergy had little or no influence, you will come upon a strange collection of local saints, as in the Celtic districts of Britain. Some of them are the descendants of Slavonic gods, whom the wily missionaries converted, willy-nilly, into respectable Christians. One of these is Vid, whose name keeps appearing in the most unlikely places, not only in Catholic Yugoslavia, but also in the Orthodox districts. Some of the older folk-songs even keep his name alive in the purely pagan form of Svetovid, and an enthusiastic painter of Belgrade even tried – unsuccessfully – to revive his pagan cult. His saint's day, Vidovdan, is very famous in Yugoslav history and has recently gained additional lustre. It was then that the Turks destroyed the last powerful coalition of the Serb and Bosnian princes under Knez Lazar on the field of Kosovo in 1389. Although independent states continued to exist for another seventy years or more after Kosovo, they were no longer powerful, and history and legend alike regard Kosovo as the downfall of the Empire of the Balkan Slavs. It was also the date of the assassination of Franz Ferdinand at Sarajevo in 1914 that started the First World War, and also of the promulgation of the pre-war Yugoslav Constitution, which was not over-popular, especially among the Croats.

In more recent times, Vidovdan marked the break between Marshal Tito and the Cominform.

The attributes of another Slavonic god, Perun, were taken over, lock, stock and barrel, by St Elias the Thunderer. For that reason you will often find the highest peak of a mountain range named after Sv. Ilija not only in Yugoslavia but also in other parts of the Balkans, such as Greece, where Slav influences were at one time or another predominant. Only Lel, the God of Love, appears to have no Christian successor.

The journey then becomes more interesting, the halts more frequent, the scenery more impressive. The boat stops at Ražanac which, from the sea, seems little more than a collection of cottages around a mediaeval castle. The quay is usually crowded – the arrival of the infrequent boats is always an occasion for the display of local beauty – and a mass of small boys eager to show their skill in swimming and diving shout at those on board to throw dinars into the water.

Here we are on territory that before the war belonged to the citizens of Zadar, where a feudal system of land-holding still prevailed. The proprietors being technically Italian, since Zadar was then an Italian enclave, the peasants did not get the benefit of the Yugoslav land reforms. They were miserably poor. Under the new administration they have presumably greater rights over the produce of the lands they till, but the whole countryside is so barren and stony that, even now, their position can hardly have improved greatly.

On the hill above Ražanac is the ancient church of St Andrija, where several of the early Croat kings were crowned. It still exists, having been respected by the Turks, who were not always so bad as patriotic historians have tried to paint them. The hill is still known as the Holy Field.

After Starigrad (one of many places called 'the old town' or fortress) and Vinjerac, the most spectacular part of the journey begins. Both are picturesque, the former with a Zrinjski-Frankopan fortress. At Starigrad the peasant boys invaded the steamer with thick bunches of wild asparagus, one of the few edible products of the barren karst. It made a welcome addition to lunch.

The last and most magnificent part of the trip is a little difficult to follow on a map. Unless it is of very large scale (like the excellent 1 : 300,000 map of the coast published in 1952 by Učila of Zagreb), the boat seems to pass over two isthmuses and then over a high range of mountains! Most ordinary maps mark Obrovac as far inland. As a matter of fact the two apparent lakes are inland seas, connected with the Mountain Channel and one another by narrow, fjord-like entrances. Through the first of these one passes into the Novigradsko More.

The last vestiges of soil disappear from the hillsides. The boat cruises slowly between shores of barren stone honeycombed with fantastic caverns. There is no sight or sound of living thing. One might be cruising on a silent sea, created before the limits of time, when God had not yet set His mind to create the beasts of the field or the flowers and green things. At the best, Leviathan might have reared his head out of the sullen waters.

It is almost with a sense of shock that one emerges into the Novigradsko More, which has, at least, fantastically twisted olives and mathematical vines, while on the farther side the ancient city and fortress of Novigrad (the 'new fortress', built about 1358) itself shows that the ages passed and man was at last created. Another equally narrow and winding channel leads into the sea of Karin.

The sea of Karin is too shallow for large ships. So we steamed across the Novigradsko More to a narrow cleft in the mountains, as dark and forbidding as that down which the luckless Persephone was haled. It was even more astounding than the gorges of the Danube, wilder and more forbidding. I wonder if Dante was ever in this part of Dalmatia? Some of the landscape has a decidedly infernal flavour.

Here the river Zrmanja enters the Novigradsko More. For almost an hour the ship moves slowly on between enormous walls of rock, so high that if one stands under the awning one cannot see the sky, but must crane outwards to look up. I wished I had been a geologist. Those rock walls must have had a story to tell. But what it was, I did not know. There is no road, no house, no sign of life; only a ruined watch-tower where, the Captain said, the Turks used to put political prisoners, and a lonely fisherman's shrine to St Nikola.

At first the only variation in the landscape was an occasional giant landfall of loose scree, another unread chapter in the geological story. Now and again the turns are so abrupt that an unskilful captain may have to back and fill, like a motor on a hairpin bend. Then for a moment one caught a glimpse of the summits of the Velebit, some of them still white with snow. The whole scene had a Himalayan grandeur.

Later on it was a little less awesome than the Novigradsko channel. There were gulls on the surface of the water, and in the distance, on the top of the rock walls, an occasional goat. Once, rounding a bend, we came upon some fishermen, who rapidly drew their boat into a fall of scree to escape our wash. If they stove it in there, it might be days before they were discovered. The sound of our engine echoed and re-echoed about the rock walls like distant giants cheering.

As we neared Obrovac, the river became a little less formidable. Once, high up on the rock wall, we caught a glimpse of the motor road, and at the foot of the cliffs were dense clusters of weeds and bullrushes that bowed to us mockingly in perfect parade order as our wash passed through them. But still no trees. Only when we were quite near the town itself did we see a few funereal cypresses guarding the cemetery, to which all corpses must be taken by boat. It must be a solemn sight to see the boats filled with mourners and chanting priests making their slow way down this devils' chasm.

This cemetery is a rare example of religious tolerance, or perhaps it is only so by necessity. For the people of this district, the Ravni Kotari, are Orthodox, whereas the coast people are Catholic. Obrovac itself is mixed.

The present administration of Yugoslavia is, of course, laic. But the old religions, or at least their tradition, still remain a living force among the country people, and the rivalry between them, though overlain, is not forgotten. One hears much of the struggles for religious freedom going on at higher levels, and especially the quarrel between the State and the Vatican, which is at least as much political as religious. But the result among the ordinary people has been a revival of religious thought, and the churches are crowded, often with young people who one would have thought would be indifferent to all such things.

A narrow path divides the cemetery; to one side lie the Orthodox under the Greek Cross, which has a smaller cross-piece at the top to mark the superscription over the head of Jesus; to the other lie the Catholics under the plain cross that we know so well.

Obrovac itself is a striking place at first sight. The canyon does not end, but simply widens out enough to allow a few fields to exist by the water's edge and three roads to converge on the little hill in the centre of the ravine in which the town is built. Needless to say, that hill is crowned by a fortress; this time it is Turkish. From it there is a magnificent view up and down the canyon of the Zrmanja.

It is also a pleasant place. The landing-stage is planted with old trees, a grateful sight to eyes wearied of stone. The girls, too, are exceptionally pretty and here wear the national dress, which is rarely to be seen now on the coast on working days. We had plenty of time to observe both, for our captain insisted on turning round before drawing in to the stage and the performance took a considerable time, bow and stern alternately touching the banks.

Now, however, the boat service is curtailed. It may only be possible to make the journey when there is a special excursion.

National dress, which I have mentioned several times in earlier pages, is now dying out. There are two main reasons for this, one the not unnatural desire of the younger people to be in the general swim and the second, and more important, its great cost. After the war, materials were in short supply and the peasants had other and more immediate things to think about. However, those who still wear it are proud of it and look natural in it. But the cost is prohibitive. A Montenegrin man's full costume may cost as much as three hundred pounds and a woman's about two hundred.

Also, national costume entails a great deal of work, which has to be subtracted from the labour in the fields. In the greater number of cases the material is home-spun and the colours are vegetable dyes that are obtained from local plants. They are, in any case, more beautiful and lasting than artificial ones. This has had the curious result that the most beautiful and complex costumes, as for example in the Ravni Kotari, come from the poorest and most barren districts, for the making of such costumes is the occupation of the women in the long winter evenings when there is little else to do. But these districts are gradually becoming depopulated, for their inhabitants find better jobs in the factories and towns, and it is not too rare to come across villages with fine stone-built houses and gardens of fruit trees where there are only a handful of people left. The older people, who have managed to preserve their costumes, often do not wear them but keep them to be buried in.

Costumes used to vary very greatly from area to area and in detail from village to village. Around Obrovac, for example, there was a predominance of red and gold. It was not too hard to recognize the main features of each national dress: the typical caps of the men from the Lika and Montenegro, the exceptionally lovely dress of the girls from the Konavle near Dubrovnik with its little patches of embroidery at the throat, the heavily embroidered boleros of Macedonia, the broidered head-scarves of Debar, the swept-back skirts of the women of the Šumadija (central Serbia), and many other distinctive forms. But to recognize the reason and origin of the various designs and to distinguish between village and village requires much time and application. Old prints and books show considerable changes in detail and design, usually towards more simplified styles, but the main features mostly remain unchanged (those who are interested in such things should compare the costumes of the Alka festival, which takes place in Sinj near Split every August, with present-day costumes; the Alka costumes are traditional and date from the early eighteenth century). Many of the costumes represent some historical event, in much the same way as the three stripes of the English blue-jacket's collar. An example of this is the 'mourning' dress of Krk, now dying out; other costumes show, in greatly conventionalized form, the crown of Dušan the Mighty or the symbols of Kosovo. The golden segment on the Montenegrin cap, for example, represents the Black Mountain, still unconquered amid the devastation of the Turkish invasions.

However, there is a good side to this ignorance of detail. During the war I made an attempt to escape from Yugoslavia on foot after the capitulation. To avoid undue attention I was wearing Serbian peasant dress, but had to get the patterned stockings which go with the dress where I could find them. Dressed thus, I was in Bijelo Polje in the Sanjak when the German armoured columns were returning from the Greek front. I was walking quietly along the road, when the leading car stopped and the

Croatian Peasant from Istria

Yugoslav National Costumes
(Photo: The Observer*)*

National
Dance,
Macedonia

colonel called me to him. My heart was in my mouth – I had been discovered! To my relief, however, all he wanted to know was where had I got my stockings. I pretended no knowledge of German and grumbled at him in Serb. The colonel cursed me and went on his way.

Luckily for me he was no expert on national dress. Had he been, my stockings would have told him that I was a virgin from Kosovo!

I have been to Zadar several times, both before and after the war. The change from Italian to Yugoslav jurisdiction has made less difference than might be supposed, but the extensive air raids the city endured during the war have made a good deal. It is true that Zadar has had its face lifted but, as in all such operations, though the former features are still recognizable, it is none the less another face.

However, this is no new experience for ancient Zadar. For centuries it was the most powerful city of Dalmatia – Dubrovnik (Ragusa) was an independent republic – and its outward aspect changed with its masters. Built on a peninsula joined by only a narrow neck to the mainland, its situation was in mediaeval times a formidable one. Zadar was supposed to have been the capital city of the Liburnians, whose shadowy annals pervade the history of all this part of Dalmatia like an unidentifiable aroma. In more historical times Zadar was the Roman Jadera, and after the fall of Salona to the Avars it became the most important city of the Roman province. It maintained this position in Byzantine and early Venetian times, with intervals of Croat rule, until it was stormed and taken by the Hungarian kings after the so-called 'personal union' with Croatia. The story of the Venetian vengeance and the diversion of the Crusaders to its reduction by the blind and venerable Doge Dandolo placed Zadar for a time in the forefront of history. For this escapade the leaders of the crusade were excommunicated by the Pope, a thunder that seems to have passed them by. In 1413 Zadar returned once more to Croato-Hungarian allegiance. This continual shifting of allegiance went on until the Turkish conquest of Hungary, when Venice was left mistress of the field. Incidentally, accounts of the crusade reveal that the unfortunate Zadar was again destroyed and sacked: 'only the churches remained'.

It was at Zadar (Zara), during the 4th Crusade, that the Soldiers of the Cross made their treaty with the exiled Emperor Alexius that led directly to the Latin sack of Constantinople.

After the First World War the fate of Zara, which became an Italian enclave in Slav Dalmatia and thereafter carried on a prosperous smuggling enterprise, was one of those serio-comic episodes that amuse one at a distance but are singularly irritating on the spot. It was also, if one reads the names of the signatories of the various petitions, a striking example of the chameleonic quality of Dalmatian family names.

I have already mentioned the desolate and ghostly impression made by Zadar shortly after the air raids, when stones from the damaged houses and the paved streets were so intermingled that it was hard to know which was which. At the time, the sight of the comparatively undamaged remains of the mediaeval city walls and the attractive sea-front seemed to transport one into another world. The impression was all the stronger because of the clear, bright Dalmatian sunlight. Such destruction and devastation seemed to go, unreasonably enough, with rain and dank skies.

But it is pleasing to know that the ninth-century Croat church of Sv. Donat has not been seriously damaged.

The statue of Grgur Ninski by Ivan Meštrović at Split

CHAPTER V

Vanished Glories: Nin, Biograd, Šibenik

Grgur Ninski, priest and patriot – Croat origins – Vanished capitals: Biograd and Nin – Bride of the Sea – The seamen of Zlarin – Šibenik cathedral – The Krka Falls – Voyage to Visovac.

The huge bronze statue of Grgur Ninski (Gregory of Nona) which used to stand in the peristyle of Diocletian's palace at Split was removed by the Italians during the last war. It was an outstanding work of art by the greatest of the Yugoslav sculptors, Ivan Meštrović. The bishop and patriot was standing in an attitude of defiance as he might well have stood in those Councils of Salona where, almost alone among the faint-hearted bishops, he defended the ancient Slavonic liturgy and the right of the people to hear divine service in a language 'understanded of the many'. His right had was raised and his long, ascetic fingers seemed ready to mark chapter and verse in the book that he held in his left hand. The Split pigeons used to settle on the book's edge as if they, too, were seeking to read, either in the book itself or in the stern countenance of the devoted champion.

It was a great work. There were many who considered it ill-placed, for Meštrović's tradition is as far as possible from the classical, and the Italians might have been forgiven for removing it elsewhere. It has now been placed in a park outside the palace walls.

This was really no more than another episode in a struggle that has been going on for over a thousand years, and spans the centuries from Grgur Ninski himself to the glagolitic manuscripts of Dom Vinko Premuda and the hostility of the rulers of Croatia and later Yugoslavia – both past and present – with the Vatican.

The episcopal seat of Grgur was at Nin, the Latin Aenona, the Italian Nona, a few miles from Zadar. Like Osor, Nin is now a city of ghosts, but in its time was one of the most important cities of Liburnia. Its fate was different from that of most of the sea-coast cities; from Roman rule it passed almost directly to Croat and became Venetian only for a short time after the Turkish invasions and the downfall of the Croato-Hungarian kingdom. Even then the Venetians paid it little heed, and after a century or two of complete stagnation it was destroyed by its Venetian masters to prevent its capture by the encroaching Turks.

Today this ancient site, the remains of whose vanished glories date back, in the form of a Bronze-Age cemetery, several centuries before Christ, is inhabited by only a few hundred peasants. Built on a tiny island, a peninsula in earlier times, it had a bad reputation for fevers. Furthermore, it has no hotels. None the less it is worth while as a day trip from Zadar, if only to remind those whose eyes have been dazzled by the beauties of Venetian architecture that for many hundred years in the past this coast was as Croatian as it is today.

Save for the Roman inscriptions, many of which have never been deciphered, the earliest written records of Nin are Croat. That over the Church of the Holy Cross reveals that it was built about the year 800 by the župan (Count or Lord-Lieutenant) Godeslav. Later, Nin became one of the capitals of the peripatetic Croat kings (as in Serbia, the capital was the residence of the ruler and therefore changed frequently) and memories of these Croat kings are multiplied up to the fourteenth century. The first Croat king known to have been a Christian, Višeslav, had his capital here in the ninth century, and in the eleventh century better-known Croat monarchs, such as Petar Krešimir and Zvonimir, held their courts at Nin. It was at Nin that the oldest known codes of Croat law were drawn up, the Statute of the District of Nin, in 1103. Naturally enough, it was in glagolitic.

Yugoslav historians have worked hard to unravel the complicated annals of the early Croat kings, that are as involved as those of England under the Heptarchy, but they still remain obscure and their names have disappeared entirely from the memories of the peasantry, to be replaced by those of Serbia, or of hajduks and uskoks, with now and again a mention of the Šubići or the more famous Bosnian rulers such as Tvrtko or Kulin Ban. It is a very curious thing. For the chanted ballads that have preserved the doings of these historical, semi-historical and sometimes purely legendary heroes are very much alive in the Ravni Kotari. But whereas any peasant would be able to tell you tales of Trajan, of Dušan the Mighty, of the dynasty of the Nemanjas, of Lazar, of Marko Kraljević, Kulin Ban, Ivo of Senj, of Karageorge, you will find none to tell you of Krešimir, Zvonimir, Godeslav, Šuronja or the great battles of the Pašman Channel, only a mile or so away. They have become meat for professors.

Only Grgur Ninski is remembered; and perhaps Meštrović has had a good deal to do with that. The Bishop of Nin was Primate of all Croatia and owed allegiance to Byzantium through Aquileia. But at the Councils of Salona the Roman Church tried to gain jurisdiction over all Dalmatia, including the Croat cities, and, by the same token, to abolish the Croat liturgy, in whose exotic and crabbed characters they smelt heresy. Details of the Councils are obscure and one-sided, but despite the vigorous defence of his people's independence by Grgur, it was Rome that won. The glagolitic liturgy was frowned upon, the ecclesiastical liberties of the Croats curtailed, and the bishopric of Nin abolished for nearly two centuries. As in most ecclesiastical controversy of the time, politics and religion were so intermingled that it was hard to say where one ended and the other began. But the sole figure of Grgur still remains in the memory as a great Croat patriot.

Roughly the same distance south of Zadar is another former Croat capital city, Biograd-na-Moru, even though its glories are visible, if at all, only to the eye of the archaeologist. I have always liked Biograd, so made it my next port of call.

Biograd has all the natural advantages. It lies on a flat plain, fertile and well-watered – and not too stony – with the snow-capped summits of the Velebit ranged like sentinels behind it. It has pleasant forests and good bathing; and the Pašman canal is perfect for sailing.

Biograd was at one time the most famous city of the Croat

littoral. But today it has the least to show for it. The present town is in reality a pleasant little Dalmatian village with scarcely an old house in it. But in the days of light sailing-ships the Pašman canal, between Biograd and the islands of Ugljan and Pašman, was the only practicable winter channel down the coast. It was the only one with any good harbours. Whoever held it, held the eastern Adriatic. Therefore it was the scene of continual sea-fighting. For 250 years, from 600 to 850, Byzantine Zadar and Croat Nin contended for it, and the whole stretch of coast from Nin down to Sukošane was known as the Graveyard. Then for 160 years the fleet of the Croat kings was the most powerful in the Adriatic and exacted tribute from all who passed through. This period of glory began with the great sea victory of Prince Mioslav in 839 and ended with the defeat of Svetoslav in a battle against the combined sea forces of Venice, Rab, Krk and Zadar in A.D. 1000. Svetoslav's brother, Šuronja, had to give territory and hostages.

It was in memory of this victory, which gave Venice the naval command of the Adriatic, that the famous ceremony of the Bucentoro was commenced. The Doge went down to the sea in his gilded barge and threw a ring into the waves, saying: 'I wed thee, O sea, in sign of our full and eternal mastery over thee.' It was carried out regularly until 1737.

A few years later, under Krešimir IV in 1059, the Croat capital was moved from land-locked Nin to open Biograd. There he built palaces and a famous monastery. It was the centre of a bishopric and the residence of the Papal Legate. It also replaced Nin as the coronation city of the Croat kings.

Croats and Venetians were then fighting for mastery of the Dalmatian coastal cities, which changed their allegiance with bewildering rapidity. But in 1123 the Venetian Doge was in Palestine, and the Croats took nearly all of them. On his return, the Doge besieged Biograd with a strong army: 'Let this infernal spot which menaces Venice be razed to its foundations.'

He literally carried out his threat. Biograd was first burnt and then systematically destroyed. Zadar, which had remained faithful to Venice, was given the island of Pašman The Bishop fled to Skradin and the citizens to Šibenik and Dolac. For 200 years the site remained waste.

It was destroyed on Good Friday 1126 – foretaste of Mussolini?
– and on Good Friday the people of Biograd still say a special
Mass and believe that a Black Knight comes out of the waves, as
he is supposed to have done on that terrible day to save the last
Croat queen who reigned in Biograd.

But Zadar later rebelled and suffered much the same fate as
Biograd, and it was on this site that the refugees founded New
Zadar. Two years later they returned to their own city, and
Biograd was known as Old Zadar – Zara Vecchia – which name
it still retains on Italian maps.

A pleasantly bibulous friend, the local professor, showed me
scraps of walls that may or may not have been part of the city
ramparts or the great cathedral church. I took his word for it.
The destruction of Biograd had been pretty thorough. But he
had unearthed at least one genuine and interesting inscription,
in glagolitic: a grant of Prince Mioslav dated 845. Incidentally
he had a theory about the Celts having greatly influenced the
Serbo-Croat language. It may be, but he rode his hobby-horse
too hard and it led him into absurdities. Still, it was strange
to find an earnest student of the Irish language in Biograd-na-
Moru.

The trip from Biograd to Šibenik lies through a maze of islands,
nearly all of them with castles or other relics of the Croat kings.
For this was the centre of the Croat naval power of the Dark Ages.
I chose to stop at Zlarin, a little outside the estuary of the Krka,
whereon lies Šibenik, and did not regret my choice.

The charms of Zlarin are of the present day. It is a quiet little
town on a quiet little island, once famous for its coral fisheries.
The people are friendly, the wine and inns are good. I went
down into the twilit courtyard to have a glass and some supper.
There were about half a dozen men at one of the tables, and I
asked if I might bring my wine over. When they heard I was
from England, three of them began to speak English with me.
For every man on Zlarin is, or has been, a sailor, and most have
served in English or American waters. Almost as many men are
overseas as are on the island itself.

The company was the best in the world: working men who
are masters of their craft, who have seen the world, and are

intelligent enough to talk about it. Most of them were islanders. There was the innkeeper, himself an old sailor, an old peasant who had been captain of a fishing-vessel on the Alaska coast, two pilots, a ship's captain, and a sergeant from the coast defence.

The conversation ranged from sea to sea, and from country to country. It scarcely touched on the two subjects of the conversationally imbecile: politics and women. A good deal of it was about fishing, in all the seven seas.

The moon rose, full and shining, flooding the courtyard with light. The wine was good and a friendly cat settled upon my knee. No evening could have passed more pleasantly.

Next morning I went to have a look at Zlarin, and the pleasant impression of the night before remained. I went over the co-operative of the coral-fishers, where every official was a fisherman, and where they worked the coral into beautiful forms with tools that might have been used by Tubal Cain.

All the women of Zlarin then wore national costume – a rare thing among the islands. And a very beautiful one it was, with black bolero over a white blouse, piped with red lanyards, a black skirt, and a brightly coloured kerchief. I tried to get a photo, but all the prettiest girls ran away when they saw the camera. I mentioned this to the innkeeper:

'Nearly all their husbands or fiancés are in America or at sea. They are afraid that if the photo is published one of them will see it and get jealous. Besides, those are not their best dresses. You should have seen them when a film company was here!'

Indeed, the women of Zlarin are extraordinary. They are proud, they are beautiful, and they are chaste. Their husbands are sometimes away for five or six years on end, but adultery is almost unheard of. They are strong too! A year or two before my last visit, they held a women's regatta here, between the women of the neighbouring islands, Zlarin, Šepurina, Žirje and Kaprije. It was no joke. The races were in heavy fishing-boats over a course of 1,500 metres!

But if the women are proud, so are the men. They consider themselves as sailors second to none, now that Perast has fallen from her high estate. They like to quote the old saying: 'First the men of Perast, then the men of Zlarin, then the men of Bakar, and then the rest.' In the days of the old Austrian Lloyd, the crack ships of the former Empire, more than half the sailors were from Zlarin.

Indeed, Zlarin is a pleasant place. I am not surprised that the nobles of Šibenik chose it as a retreat when their city was ravaged by the plague and only 1,500 souls were left alive. What a Decameron it must have been! But, alas, there was no Boccaccio.

From Zlarin to Šibenik one goes by caïque in about half an hour. The city lies on an arm of the sea that is really the estuary of the river Krka. The narrow entrance is guarded by the beautiful old Venetian fortress of St Nikola, built after the plans of the famous Leonardo Sammichele in 1546. It, too, is an island. Sammichele was not only an excellent military engineer, but also something of an artist, and it is interesting to contrast its beautiful lines with the stark utility of fortresses like Knin or Klis.

I recommend everyone to spend at least a day in Šibenik to see the cathedral. For more than a hundred years the cathedral was at once the pride and the bane of the people of Šibenik. They poured out all their treasures to complete it, but grumbled all the time that it would bankrupt them, which it nearly did. The foundation was laid in 1431, and the exterior was considered finished in 1536.

It is in various styles, according to the tastes of the architects who succeeded one another through the century of construction. But they are so perfectly harmonized that only the architect is aware of this; the cathedral is most definitely a unit and not a patchwork. The first architect, Francesco da Giacomo, did little save make mistakes, and was removed after ten years' work. The second, Giorgio Orsini of Zadar, who was known, like all Slav artists of the time, as Schiavone, built in decorated Venetian Gothic; whereas the third architect of the building, Niccolo the Florentine, completed it in the Tuscan renaissance style. Most of their assistants were local craftsmen.

The main doorway is the Lion Gate, which represents the entry into Paradise and is flanked by two lions which watch the gateway with amiable smiles. No sinner would give up hope in face of such guidance. Above them, in niches, are delightfully prudent statues of Adam and Eve driven from Paradise. Above

The Lion Gate of the cathedral at Šibenik

them again are Saints Peter and Paul, masterpieces of fifteenth-century carving by Giorgio Orsini himself. On each side of the door are richly decorated columns, some with conventional designs of leaves and flowers, others, more ambitious, where birds and beasts chase one another in eternal pursuit. Yet others have tiny medallions with heads of famous men. Some of these were badly damaged, and a nineteenth-century restorer added those of Victor Emmanuel, Garibaldi and Mazzini! The whole has the life and the intricacy of an Indian temple, but with a grace, a harmony and a symmetry that could be only Latin in origin. The portal was finished about 1438.

A superb frieze of seventy-one heads encircles the outer wall of the apse. It is a carven history of Dalmatia in stone. Every head is different and every head has character. There you will find girls' heads of classical beauty, fierce Slavs with long moustaches and high cheek-bones like the Ličani of the present day, shaven Turkish warriors, Byzantines, Italians, Tatars, nobles, lawyers, priests and laymen. One knight has had his nose amputated, a common punishment of mediaeval times. Another, an Italian condottiere probably, is astonishingly like Mussolini. Others you will still see today, walking in the market-place. All are little masterpieces of wit and of beauty. From the three dark corners ferocious lions glare.

In the interior of the cathedral many details have the humour of the Gothic. One column, in a darkened corner, is decorated with two cherubs' heads. The one turned towards the interior of the church is singing praises with happy, fat-cheeked face; the other turned towards the shadowy wall has the staring eyes, the quivering lips and the tear-stained face of a child afraid of the dark.

And of course the roof, which is of stone barrel-vaulting. Indeed, the whole cathedral, including the roof and dome, is of stone, an astonishing feat of technique considering the size of the building and the period in which it was built. The main portal also is magnificent, though the two sculpture niches are still empty. After spending millions of ducats on their cathedral, the people of Šibenik had not enough money left to pay for the statues.

Everyone who visits Šibenik makes an excursion to the falls of the Krka. Thither I, too, decided to go, but also decided to combine it with an excursion to the island cloister of Visovac.

It was an expensive and rather complicated journey, as I had to hire a motor launch to reach the island of Visovac. The tourist agency got it for me, however, and then told me that an English lady also wished to visit Visovac. Would I mind if she shared the expenses and the facilities? I never mind meeting new people, and said I would call for her the next morning.

When I got to her hotel a vigorous old lady appeared. It would be ungallant of me to guess how old. Let us say that I was surprised to see her travelling so far from home. But she had a gallant spirit and made little of the wearisomeness of the journey, which I am afraid I exaggerated somewhat. Let me say at once, however, that she proved a very charming travelling companion.

The people of the Continent like to laugh at these vigorous old Englishwomen. Their appearance often gives good cause. But they make a great mistake. There is often more brains and character in their little fingers than in all the fluffy pates of Vienna. Often they have spent their golden years in the wild places of the world; one whom I met had spent eighteen years on the Canadian prairies, another ten years in organizing a Turkish university, another half a lifetime keeping camp for her husband in the mountains of Ecuador and Peru. May I add another tribute to their hardly-won laurels.

The river was low and therefore the Krka Falls not at their best. But none the less they were fine. The river spreads out first into a wide lake, dotted with countless islands, looking from above like the pieces of a green jigsaw puzzle scattered haphazard on a brilliant blue cloth. The stony mountains around heighten the colour and the contrast. Then they gather themselves together and the river forms a single stream, to leap irresistibly downwards in terraced silver cascades 300 feet wide. The total fall is about 130 feet, the air is filled with spray, and groaning thunder echoes from the hills; just below the falls the river again widens into the smooth and placid Gulf of Skradin.

We lingered for some time, watching the rush of water. Fruit trees, watered by the spray, clung to little cornices in the rocks. The figs especially bear well, but it will be a bold man who gathers them. But time was pressing, and we went back to our motor-boat with ears still deafened by the falls.

We plugged our way asthmatically against the current. The river here is more like a series of lakes opening one out of another and quite silent, save for the cries of a few water-birds and the chugging of our engine. After the falls, there is not a house in sight.

In the third reach we saw the island cloister of Visovac. The building was modern but dignified, with its church tower matching in height the tall fringe of poplars along the banks. It seemed a perfect spot for rest and meditation, though in fact the monks lead a busy enough life.

We were welcomed graciously, with true monastic hospitality. The permanent staff of the monastery is small: four brothers, thirteen novices and some servants. There are usually a number of guests, priests retiring after the troubles of their cures.

There is not a great deal to be seen in the church and monastery. The settlement dates from 1445 when it was occupied by Paulician hermits, but they were soon replaced after the Turkish invasions by Bosnian Franciscans. The monastery was built in 1576, but was destroyed by the Turks and the monks forced to flee in 1648. In 1675 they again returned. The present buildings date from 1725, but have been several times repaired. There are a few valuable books in the library.

Incidentally, the popular derivation of the name Visovac from 'visiti', to hang, because the Turks are said to have hanged the monks on their own trees, is a pious invention. The name is older than the Turkish invasion and is probably connected with the nearby falls. Besides, it would be very difficult to hang a number of men on a poplar or a cypress, and there were no other trees.

Its isolated situation made the monastery a refuge for all sorts of brigands and outlaws in the disturbed times of Dalmatia. These were recalled only too recently, for during the last war Visovac was often used as a hide-out for members of the resistance – or their opponents.

CHAPTER VI

Pleasures and Palaces: Split

*The Serbian cuisine – Palace of Diocletian – Salona – Early Christian
archaeology – The fortress of Klis – Riviera of the Seven Castles – Yugoslav
folk-songs – Background to Trogir – Snakes and oxen.*

Since World War I Split has become one of the busiest ports of
the Mediterranean. Its growing prosperity is reflected in the
growth of its population, which has increased steadily since
1918. If it had better rail communications with its hinterland, it
would soon become a major port. As it is, Yugoslav development
plans have shied off putting additional strain on the Zagreb–Lika
line to Split and have concentrated on developing Rijeka and on
the creation of fresh Adriatic outlets at Ploče and Bar.

The reason for this economic digression is to speak of restaurants.
Split, being a comparatively large city, has a number of restaurants
where the typical Serbian, as distinct from Dalmatian, cuisine
can be sampled. It is excellent, being a combination of the best
features of the Balkan and Hungarian cuisines with some distinctive features of its own, but with a basis of pork rather than the
somewhat greasy mutton which so often spoils the best efforts of
Greek and Turkish cooks.

But it is rather heavy. Therefore those who sample it in the
heat of Dalmatia would be well advised to do so at dinner rather
than at lunch and to counteract its heaviness with plenty of good
local red wine.

The most popular Serbian dishes are ćevapčići and ražnjići.
The former are small rolls of mixed minced pork and beef (mainly
pork), like small skinless sausages, cooked over a charcoal grill.
These grills are often outside the restaurant, where the smell of
the grilling is a most pleasant and persuasive advertisement. Since
the war, the size of the average ćevapčić has grown smaller; at

present, ten make a good meal. They are usually served with chopped raw onion, but real connoisseurs will often ask for them served with kajmak, another Serbian delicacy not unlike a double-cream cheese.

Ražnjići are small pieces of pork (sometimes alternating with veal) threaded on a skewer and also cooked over a charcoal grill. They are a local and simplified version of the well-known Caucasian shashlik. They, too, are eaten with raw onion.

Frequently these delicacies are served in small restaurants which specialize in grills and often sell nothing else – except, of course, rakija and wine. The number of variations on the basic theme of grill is legion. Pleskavica is meat minced as for ćevapčići and grilled in small rissoles together with onion and hot peppers. This sounds rather like an ordinary hamburger, but the charcoal grill gives it a special flavour of its own.

The spit, in fact, might be called the armoury of the Balkan cook. His masterpieces are sucking-pig and young lamb roasted on the spit. And when I say young, I mean young. The whole pig or lamb is seldom more than eighteen inches long, and the result is meat so delicate in flavour as to be almost unrecognizable after the tough, stringy scrags we have for so long eaten in England. Incidentally, the sight of the young sucking-pig on the spit is sometimes surprising to those who have never seen it before. Once in Sarajevo, a Bosnian friend and myself almost caused an international incident over sucking-pig. A party of German tourists saw one and asked the world at large, 'What is that?' My Bosnian friend, in a stage whisper, said 'Baby!' The Germans left.

Among the regular dishes, the sarma has pride of place. It consists of a stuffing of rice and minced pork wrapped in cabbage leaves, preferably soured, and cooked very slowly and for a long time with smoked gammon and ribs of pork. Sarmas are usually served very hot; if the cabbage leaves are sweet, then they are served with yoghourt or sour cream. A variant is the sarma of vine leaves. These are smaller and the meat usually mutton; they are also served hot with sour cream. A Greek variant, some-times to be found in Dalmatia, is to serve them cold with lemon sauce. They are seasonal, since the vine leaves must be tender and without the hard fibres which develop in them when the grapes themselves are ripe.

Stuffed peppers, tomatoes or small marrows are all good stand-bys.

Care should be taken with the Bosnian stew (Bosanski lonac). It is rather like a Lancashire hot-pot, and the basic meat is mutton. But the large white things in the stew are not always, as one might suppose, potatoes; often they are whole heads of garlic. This is somewhat disconcerting to English culinary adventurers.

On the other hand, a dish to be highly recommended is djuveč, a thick rice casserole with peppers, tomatoes, aubergines and string beans with a basis of pork. It is exceedingly rich and very good. It is flavoured with hot paprika, and those who do not like hot dishes would be well advised to find out how much. Djuveč can also be made with game, though rarely in Dalmatia, or with fish, usually carp. This last is a question of taste; for my own part I do not think much of it.

Podvarak is meat, poultry, usually goose or turkey, or game roasted over shredded cabbage in such a way that the meat-juices fall on to the cabbage and give it additional flavour. It is very good. Rezanci is only the local name for noodles.

Papazjanija is merely spring-onion stew with a funny name; while ajmokac is also stew, being the Slav corruption of the German *eingemacht*.

There are also several excellent local versions of paprikashes and goulashes, Hungarian dishes that have become naturalized. Their main flavour is sweet red paprika, which most people like.

A standard Yugoslav dish is pasulj, which merely means beans. The beans are cooked with smoked pork and hot red paprikas for a very long time until all the flavours become pleasantly fused. But it is too heavy for a hot climate such as that of Dalmatia. Pasulj is frequently served in the Serbian and Macedonian monasteries, where the amount of hot paprika is sometimes surprising. I recall being 'honoured' with pasulj at the very isolated monastery of Matejić on the mountains overlooking the plain of Kumanovo in Macedonia. It was very good pasulj and I was very hungry. But it was so highly seasoned that the sweat poured down my forehead in streams as I ate it, much to the amusement of the sole resident monk and a group of the monastery's Albanian goatherds.

Incidentally, if you arrive at a monastery in times of fast – and they are many in the Orthodox Church – you may get your pasulj *posni* – fasting and without meat. This is rather dull.

In those restaurants where they are used to foreign guests one may also sometimes find old friends under names which have suffered some surprising changes. Sometimes it requires a good deal of philological concentration to recognize them. One which caused me a good deal of trouble was ajrišću – it turned out to be Irish stew. Another and more familiar one is emeneks – ham and eggs.

A local salad which is excellent is ajvar. It is made of cooked sweet peppers and aubergines minced together and served with hot pepper – according to taste – lemon juice, salt, oil and garlic. Most cooks will vary the proportions to the taste of the customer.

Two other excellent and somewhat similar highlights of the Yugoslav cuisine must also be mentioned – pita and burek. Pita is made with the paper-thin oriental pastry that has about the same relation to ordinary *millefeuilles* as a spider's web to a ball of string; it is served in more or less familiar form. Burek is much thicker, and usually baked on huge copper trays and cut into segments. In Bosnia, but rarely elsewhere, it is made in long rolls. Between the countless leaves of thin pastry, brown and crisp from the oven, there is a thick layer of filling, either savoury or sweet. The most usual savoury fillings are soft cheese or minced meat; the most usual sweet ones are apple, dark cherries or pumpkin; this last, being very cheap, is usually sold by itinerant vendors at street corners.

Since the war it has become increasingly difficult to find good restaurants specializing in national dishes, except of course in the big cities. So it is pleasant to report an exceptionally good one. It is at Žarovište, a mountain overlooking the bay of Cavtat and the city of Dubrovnik. The view is magnificent, the surroundings rural and the food well and carefully prepared. The only disadvantage is that it is several kilometres from the centre of the town and, if you do not have a car, it is necessary to take a taxi there. If you do, get the driver to wait and bring you back behind the mountains and down the valley of the Ombla – the Dubrovačka Rijeka (River of Dubrovnik).

Of the many Dalmatian fish I have spoken earlier; those of the Danube and the lakes I have dealt with in a later chapter. But there is one branch I overlooked; the squids and octopods. These somewhat unpleasant looking objects are cooked in a variety of ways. Frequently they are fried as *meze* to be eaten as snacks with rakija. Generally speaking, the squids (kalamari) taste like delicate inner tube, the octopods like outer tube. Once I even found a Rhodes cat – the most famished of its kind – who could not deal with fried octopus. But a risotto of young kalamari, crisply fired and not more than three inches long, served in their own ink, is a colourful and satisfying dish.

Split owes its name and its existence to the palace of Diocletian. The name is probably a contraction of εἰσ τόν παλατιόν – Spalato – Split. And throughout the Middle Ages, the palace actually *was* Split – there are still about 300 houses within its walls – so that his mighty presence dominated the life of the city. The visitor's first thought is of Diocletian.

Since the war the clearing of Diocletian's palace has been speeded up; a number of vistas have been opened and some of the later buildings that cluttered up the interior have been removed. Also, an extensive system of cellars has been discovered and excavated. As a result, one comes upon the palace with a slight shock of familiarity. Today, it far more closely resembles Robert Adam's eighteenth-century drawings, and it is with pleasure that one recognizes many details characteristic of the Adam style. Unfortunately, as the palace renews its youth, the Adelphi is being destroyed.

Adam was here in 1757, a few years before Fortis, and made detailed drawings of the palace, which later became the basis for the Adam style. But his investigations drew upon him the suspicions of the Venetian authorities – how modern that sounds! —and he was put into prison as a spy, whence he escaped only by the intervention of the Venetian commandant, Robert Graeme. That name interests me. How did a Graeme come to such a position? Perhaps he was an adherent of the Stuarts

The Porta Aurea of the palace of Diocletian at Split

who had fled after the '15 or the '45? But no one could tell me.

There is little point in describing the remains of the palace. That is done very effectively by a number of publications easily obtainable on the spot, in many languages. But since most visitors come to Split by boat, it is worth recalling, as an aid to the imagination, what the great seaward portico must have looked like in the days of its glory. For one thing, the 'molo' is new. The portico, with its enormous line of columns, rose on a heavy base directly from the shore, the whole about 70 feet high. It was about 600 feet long and flanked by two large square towers, one of which still exists. Behind the columns was a great hall, decorated with mosaics, looking seaward and opening on to the Imperial apartments. Truly this scene of Imperial splendour was worthy of the description: 'the noblest dwelling-place ever erected for a single man'.

The palace was built between 285 and 305. Its architecture has become the subject of a violent dispute between professors, into which I have no desire to intrude: one school considers it the decadence of the Roman style, a view supported by the crudeness of some of the detail; the other considers it the birthplace of Byzantine and Romanesque architecture, a view supported by many architectural details and the bold abandonment of many features considered necessary by Vitruvius.

Diocletian lived there until 313. It then seems to have passed into a period of shadow, having apparently become a military store. Its next appearance in history was when Julius Nepos, pretender to the Empire and more or less Caesar of Dalmatia, was murdered there in 480. It was damaged but not sacked by the Avars, who destroyed Salona, and then became the refuge of the Salonitans.

After a long period of turbulence, during which Split passed from Byzantine to Croat and Venetian rulers and back again, the city finally emerges in the Middle Ages as an autonomous municipality, more powerful than most of its nominal overlords. In 1390 its overlord was the most famous of the Bosnian kings, Stefan Tvrtko, and in 1403 it was under his general, Hrvoje Vukčić, who remained until 1413 and made himself thoroughly unpopular. One of the towers in the 'burgus', or mediaeval town, just outside the palace and near the flower-market, is attributed to Hrvoje, though a Venetian lion was later added to it. On his disgrace the people sang a Mass of thanksgiving for their deliverance from Pharaoh. But this may have been due to his leanings towards the Bogumil heresy, for they had little real cause to regret him. Without his strong rule, Split lost much land and power and in 1420 surrendered to the Venetians or, according to some historians, suffered the indignity of being sold to them for 100,000 ducats.

Through the sixteenth and seventeenth centuries Split, under Venetian governors, had her hands full in defending herself against the Turks, especially after the fall of Klis, and had little time for civil strife. The Turkish frontier was on the Jadar, only a mile or so away from the city. After the fall of the Venetian republic in 1797 she had the same history as the rest of Dalmatia.

Yet, despite the mighty shadow of Diocletian, Split is essentially a city of the present. It is the greatest port in Dalmatia and serves as a magnet to the islanders who form the most energetic part of its population. It is, for the visitor, mainly a place of passage. Yet one lingers in it and the days slip by unnoticed. One does nothing very much, save watch the wheeling swallows in the Central Square, or stroll up and down the molo, where the sailing-boats form a floating market, selling wine and oil and fruit from planks hung out over their sterns. Yet one's days seem full of incident. For the people of Split are gay, carefree and eternally rebellious. They were among the first to rally to the cry of united Yugoslavia and among the most determined defenders of her independence in the partisan wars. They are always either singing or protesting. Split is as unstable in temperament as the waters of its harbour. It has many of the less pleasing aspects of a great port, yet it remains aristocratic. And its surroundings are still worthy of the retirement of an emperor.

It is possible that St Jerome came from somewhere near Split. It would explain his splenetic temper and his heartfelt repentance:

'Pardon me, O Lord, for I am a Dalmatian!'

Salona is not far from Split and was, in classical times, far the greater city. Indeed, Split was only the palace; the classical site was Epetion, the modern Stobreč.

Salona was an important city, with a population estimated at between 40,000 and 60,000. It has been celebrated by many classical writers, including Lucan, whose lines:

> Qua maris Adriatici longas ferit unda Salonas
> Et tepidum in molles zephyros excurrit Iader

no writer, including myself, has been able to omit. It was mentioned by Constantine Porphyrogenitos as being half as large as Constantinople itself. That, I fear, was an exaggeration, but it gives a measure of its importance. Its great period began after the civil war, when it had luck or foresight enough to hold for Caesar against Pompey, and under Augustus the Colonia Martia Julia Salonae was one of the leading cities of the Empire. More important for the archaeologist, it was one of the greatest centres of early Roman Christianity, and because of its early destruction its monuments have not been overlaid by those of more recent piety. They date from, roughly, the end of the third century, the epoch of Venantius and Domnius, to the beginning of the seventh, when Salona was destroyed. That is a rare period, so Salona has a great reputation. It is probably the finest site yet discovered for early Roman Christianity.

That is, indeed, the main advantage of discoveries in the Balkans over those in Greece and Italy. For the Greeks and Romans rebuilt their cities and continued to live in them, whereas the nomad Slavs and Avars, who destroyed the classical civilization of the Balkans, usually left the sites waste and built their villages elsewhere. So that such damage as has been done since their destruction has been done by time, by amateur archaeologists, or by peasants requiring building material. Often the sites have been entirely forgotten and covered with earth, only awaiting excavation. At the worst, one may find a few cottages at or near the site, usually with some such name as Zlokućani (the evil houses) or Gradište (the buildings), &c. The same is, of course, true of such British sites as Verulamium, which is some way from mediaeval St Albans, but Britain was a wild and distant province, whereas the Balkans were the bridge between Greece and Italy, were highly civilized, and, under the Claudians, were the centre of the Roman Empire.

Salona was, from the archaeological point of view, twice destroyed: once by the Avars in the seventh century, who left it ruined, but more or less intact, and again by the Venetians, who feared lest the ruins might shelter Turkish raiding bands. The second destruction was, archaeologically, the more regrettable.

One of the reasons for the importance of Salona was that it was situated at the seaward opening of the great gorge that leads through the fastnesses of the Mosor mountains into the interior, to Klis, Sinj and the Illyrian fortress of Knin (Arduba), famous in the Roman occupation for the fierce defence of its people and the voluntary sacrifice of its women, who, like the Suliotes, threw themselves down the cliffs to death rather than accept captivity. Klis is easily visible from Salona.

The road is guaranteed to make any tapeworm giddy. I remember crawling up it in an ancient Chevrolet to see the tournament of the Alka at Sinj, where on August 16th every year the local peasants hold a jousting match in mediaeval costume to commemorate the great defeat of the Turks in 1715. Klis was for centuries one of the key positions of the Balkans.

It was the fortress of Petar Kružić, whose tomb we have seen at Trsat. As a fortress it was impregnable, secure against everything save famine or treachery. Even against artillery it would be a formidable barrier. Range after range of ramparts encircle the hill, till they culminate in the citadel on the summit. Nowadays there is a road to the outer gate whereas before it was well-nigh unapproachable.

On the summit there is almost always a fresh breeze, a pleasant coolness after the warmth of the low-lying sea-coast villages. Behind, is the pass to Sinj, a narrow channel between bare mountains; before, the gorge widens out until it loses itself in the fertile plain of the Splitsko Polje and the Riviera of the Seven Castles. A little to the left is Split itself and the wooded hillside park of Marjan, where once Diocletian had his hunting-grounds. Then the harbour-works and Vranjic, like a tiny Venice, in the centre of the bay. Then the trout-filled Jadar and the ruins of Salona and, beyond them, the fertile villages of the Seven Castles and distant Trogir. Immediately below is the modern village of Klis. Far out to sea stretch the islands. One can see an incredible distance:

beyond Čiovo and Brač and rosemary-scented Šolta to Hvar and even, vaguely perceived, far-distant Vis. It is a view that surpasses all superlatives.

The grim ramifications of the fortress itself are full of an awesome and sombre charm. Time has softened their outlines and filled the crannies with wild rosemary, sweet-scented salvia and lavender. On the very summit is a church that was once a Turkish mosque, but the minaret has gone. In the citadel are rooms, used until the First World War as prisons for political prisoners. The windows, if one may use such a term for wide stone embrasures, are unbarred. I climbed on the sill of one and looked down. Bars were unnecessary. Below was a sheer rock wall of 400 or 500 feet.

The road from Split through Salona to Trogir is one of the loveliest in Dalmatia. It is also one of the best. It passes through the Riviera of the Seven Castles, a number of little villages that are ideal for a quiet summer holiday. The remnants of the seven castles themselves – they are Venetian – are just enough to give a pleasant flavour of the past to these little resorts whose charm is of the present; bathing, fishing, and boating in the clear waters of the gulf and, in the evenings, gatherings in the tiny local kafanas, notable for their excellent wine. The hotels are pleasant, in keeping with the villages themselves. I have passed many an evening listening to the young people of the villages – one cannot call them peasants, for there is here a long tradition of culture and good breeding – singing the songs of Dalmatia and of Split itself.

There is nothing that so recalls a scene as a smell. Even today I cannot smell crushed mint without remembering evenings outside the little kafana at Kaštel Stari, where it grew close to the doorway and was trodden down by each incoming guest. In the soft, velvety air of the Dalmatian night, the scent hung almost palpably. A few feet in front of us the waves broke in little flashes of phosphorescence like a line of fire along the shore. Behind us, the life of the village murmured on in old courts and doorways like a half-heard melody against the *strillo ostinato* of crickets in the vineyards and olive-groves.

And we sang; sometimes the proud song of Split:

'Ča je pusta Londra kontra Splitu gradu'
(What is mighty London compared with Split the city)

and sometimes the famous song of Dubrovnik, 'Adio Mare', which is not, as one might suppose, a farewell to the sea but to a young lady called Mary; or the lovely song from one of Tijardović's operettas 'Daleko mi moj Split' (My Split is far from me), which has become so popular and is so frequently sung that, despite its enormous range, it almost ranks as a folk-song.

These Dalmatian songs are a good introduction to the rich folk-music of Yugoslavia. For they are easy on the European ear and use the familiar scale. They have been strongly influenced by the music of Italy, but have a melancholy seldom to be found in Italian songs (now and again one hears a real Italian song translated and sung, and then the difference is apparent). In Bosnia, Serbia and Macedonia the melodies are far more complex, grace-notes and quarter-tones are common, as also wailing portamenti, and they often use the oriental scale with the sharpened seventh. Their charm grows on one, especially when they are sung to the local and primitive instruments, and little by little one comes to prefer them to their smoother and more familiar counterparts of the coastlands or Slovenia.

The road through the Seven Castles leads to the town of Trogir. Trogir is perhaps the best example existing of a mediaeval city that has passed through little or no outward change from the days of its glory to the present time. Once through its gateways the noise of traffic is left behind and one drops at once into mediaeval days, with all their charm intact but without their disadvantages of faction, strife and recurrent pestilence. It has the attraction of a fairy-tale that is independent of time and place. For myself, I like it best after the almonds have been gathered and the inhabitants sit in the narrow, stone-paved streets outside their doorways cracking the shells with tiny hammers and sorting the nuts into woven baskets. Then it sounds like a Nibelung chorus.

Trogir has an ancient history. It was a Greek colony of the third century B.C., and professors still argue whether its name is derived from a goat or, because of the shape of the island on which it is built, a water-melon. It doesn't matter. For four centuries it was part of a Byzantine theme and for five under Croat or Croato-Hungarian kings. During this period it withstood an attack by the Tatars. They could not cross the narrow channel

which then separated it from the mainland. They were chasing
the fugitive King Bela IV. The burghers of Trogir were, however,
more stout-hearted than their ruler, who fled still farther, to a
tiny island out at sea which still bears the name Kraljevac (from
Kralj – king). In the fifteenth century it fell to Venice, though
Venetian historians somewhat wryly complain that the common
people insisted on retaining their Croat customs, costumes and
language, and remained so until the fall of the Serenissima in 1797.

To try to summarize the history and attractions of Trogir is too
big a task for a butterfly writer whose aim is to touch lightly and
then pass on. In any case, it has been excellently done in a booklet
on Trogir edited by Jerko Čulić, a friend of mine for many years,
whose knowledge and love for Dalmatia were unequalled, and
whose untimely death was a great blow to lovers of this land. It
is rather indigestible reading in England, but it is invaluable –
and obtainable – on the spot. But perhaps it is better to sit for a
moment in the little square in front of the cathedral, where the
centuries of Trogir meet and mingle, and look at the magnificent
portal of the cathedral before one. It is dated and signed: in 1240
by the master Radovan, 'the most excellent in this art'. Adam and
Eve stand, one on each side of the portal, upon two lions; one is
killing a dragon and the other has a lamb in its claws, but the
Gothic tradition is such that they are, none the less, gentle and
amiable beasts.

Incidentally, the Latin inscription *per Radovanum Crohatis ante
predam aut pertinet ex Christi culturis exagliphis* has been amusingly
misread, so that many people believe that this doorway was
carved by Christians before the Croatian conquest of Trogir in
639 and was brought here in 1240!

Another aside. For those who like philological curiosities, the
cathedral itself is filled with rhyming inscriptions in mediaeval
Latin that read, at the present day, most amusingly.

Trogir's Croat tradition has always irritated the more chauvin-
istic of the Italians, especially in fascist times. Between the wars,
fascist propaganda that 'wherever there is a winged lion there is
Italy' caused the Yugoslavs to remove these Venetian symbols,
and started that seriocomic episode of the Lion of Trogir that even
disturbed the august councils of the League of Nations. I do not

want to go too deeply into this controversy. But it is worth while remembering that the original insult was Venetian. The inscription in the book of the great winged lion in the Loggia, dated 1471 (it is not destroyed, but preserved in the Municipal Museum), was not the usual *Pax tibi, Marce, evangelista meus,* but *Iniusti punienter et semen irripiorum peribit.* During the last war the Italians in 1941 removed the statue of the Croat hero Berislavić, another work by Meštrović, which stood in the Loggia and, worse barbarism still, set themselves systematically to destroy all traces of Trogir's Croat past.

Needless to say, after such treatment and with such a tradition, the people of Trogir took a leading part in the partisan wars.

The ridiculous, however, is not limited to modern times. The island of Čiovo, on the seaward side of the tiny island on which Trogir is built, was known in classical times as Boas, since it was believed that large snakes lived there which ate oxen! Čiovo is a pleasant island, as is also Šolta, famous according to Pliny for its plantations of rosemary. But both were used by the Roman Emperors as places of political exile and afterwards for the removal from circulation of prominent heretics. One must believe either that the Emperors were not as cruel as tradition would have us believe, or, more reasonable and more likely, that they had never seen the islands and had no idea what they were like. Or perhaps they were thinking of those snakes!

CHAPTER VII

Pirates and Wines: Omiš and the Islands

Descendants of the Liburnians – The pirates of Omiš – A walk through Brač – The Petrinović mausoleum – Two great sculptors – Meštrović and Rosandić—The wines of Vis—Kafana names—Miracles at Komiža— Hvar – The Moreška at Korčula – Pirates and pelicans.

A boat like a Liburnian galley, descendant of the ancient pirates, is entering the harbour of Omiš. I have stopped to look at it and to wonder how anyone could possibly live in a little house half-way up the great stone rampart of Biokovo.

Omiš was a pirate stronghold. But all the pirates have gone now, or perhaps they have all turned taxi-drivers in Dubrovnik. But it doesn't matter. They have left their mark on Omiš, which is doubtless more comfortable for their absence.

Those villages, for instance. The older ones are far up the hillside, out of reach of retaliatory raids, with watch-towers to give the alarm. Only the fortified towns and the more recent settlements are on the sea-shore. Omiš itself, for example. No one dared to attack it for decades. The Venetians spent many millions of ducats in an attempt to dislodge it, and a Senator remarked that they would willingly have paid as many more to have kept their fingers unburnt. The people of Omiš were the successors to the pagan Neretljani, and after their final suppression the pirate tradition moved northwards to Senj. Under the Kačić family they played the racketeers' game, too, exacting money for the protection of the commerce of Kotor, Split and Dubrovnik to let their ships pass in peace. There are several treaties of the twelfth century to prove the fact; and in 1221 the Pope himself preached a holy war against them for plundering the ships of the Crusaders. Only in 1444 were they forced to yield to the Venetians, as one of the last independent cities of Dalmatia.

Omiš was always a pirate town. She had little trade and little truck with the trappings of nobility. In the whole city I could see only one coat-of-arms, and that the Bishop's. I asked the parish priest how he reconciled bishops with piracy, but he merely shrugged his shoulders and remarked that they had different ideas in the Middle Ages. Their clergy, too, were a tough lot. They used the cryptic Bosnian script up to the early nineteenth century and were not free from suspicion of the Bosnian heresy. We might say of them today that they had leanings towards Bolshevism. The priest showed me a magnificent silver-gilt thirteenth-century Italian ostensorium. It was loot from the Benedictine Abbey of Tremiti, acquired by typical mediaeval treachery. The sea-raiders asked the monks to give one of their members Christian burial. But the man in the coffin was alive and with him were the weapons of the band. Once within the abbey, the dead man arose and armed his fellows and the massacre began.

The pirates chose their lair well. It controls the traffic through the Korčula canal. Though Omiš is today a pleasant little place of tree-lined avenues, it lies at the mouth of the Cetina gorge, where all the pirate fleets in the world could lie at anchor. From the landward side it is almost inaccessible.

The modern road turns abruptly into the gorge. I went to look at it. It was very still and quite deserted. Across the river was a tiny church and two or three cottages, but no sign of inhabitants. There was not a sound, save the tinkle of a distant waterfall from a great height and the croaking of innumerable frogs, treble and bass answering each other in antiphony. A little farther on were rich water-meadows, unapproachable save by boat, and huge masses of bright purple flowers of which I did not know the name. I carried some of them about with me for days, but when at last I met a knowledgeable botanist they were already beyond hope of identification.

There are six kilometres of navigable river here, almost in-accessible, save by sea, before the road was built. No pirates could have found a better haven.

In these desolate mountains was the tiny peasant republic of the Poljice. But all traces of it have long vanished, and those interested in its curious political customs, which recall those of the pre-Carolingian Franks, I refer to Fortis, Lučić or other historians.

Despite their Bishop, who incidentally lived for most of the time at Makarska, Christianity sat very lightly on the people of Omiš and the Poljice. Their predecessors, the Neretljani, remained pagan until the ninth century, long after the rest of the Slavs were converted, and the people of the Primorje ('littoral' – a generic term, but locally used to mean the sea-coast from Omiš to the mouth of the Neretva) clung to their ancient beliefs and, even when converted, were considered tainted with heresy.

The old gods still reigned under new names. Fortis mentions that 'the shepherds of Poglizza have a particular devotion for St Vito' (Vid), and also refers to a Perun Dubrava or Grove of Perun.

There is also a Vidov Gora on the island of Brač, where I went next day. Conformant to so great a saint or deity – have it which way you will – it is the highest point on the island, and there was almost certainly a grove there at some time.

Brač is the largest of the islands of Dalmatia and one of the least known and most charming. Little is known of its history. Pliny mentions the excellence of its goats'-milk cheese – *capris laudata Brattia* – and Fortis the excellence of its wines. Near Splitska the foundations of a third-century basilica have been found. There are some Venetian remnants. That is about all.

I determined to walk across the island from Sumartin, where I landed, to Povlje and eventually Supetar.

That walk was one of the most difficult and most beautiful of my life. Brač does not show her most attractive side to the sea. The shores are bare and rocky, with scarcely a trace of vegetation save in the sheltered bays where are the villages. The winter bura sees to that.

But away from the exposed sea-shore it is different. The paths are narrow and made of rough stone that tears the very soles out of one's boots. One's feet suffer, but one's heart is filled with colour and gaiety. It was a feast-day and there was no one in the fields; the only sign of man was a plane zooming overhead. Bright-green lizards, with quivering tails, were sunning themselves on the hot stones. The stone walls themselves were bright with yellow broom and the peculiarly rich, velvety flame of the pomegranate blossoms. The fields were either laid out with drill-room vines or with gruesomely contorted olives; the one looking like new recruits training for war, the other like aged veterans bent and twisted in its service. The fat, bulbous figs seemed aggressively conscious of their fruitfulness, like the figures in Botticelli's *Primavera*. Sometimes I came to a patch of raw stone with only the inevitable rosemary and salvia to give it life. Then I would crush the leaves and walk on, refreshed by their fragrance. Sometimes I would look down at some sheltered sea-cove, blue and still, with a tiny village at the water's edge.

I cannot describe all the villages of Brač that I passed through on that walk. It was a long one and took me a couple of days; I spent the night at Selca, a village of stonemasons. The quarries of Brač have been famous since the days when Diocletian used its stone for his palace. Even before, for there are many traces of Iron- and Bronze-Age man on the island. Trogir Cathedral, too, is made of Brač stone, as well as many famous buildings throughout the world, for there is, or was, a considerable export trade. It possesses the curious quality, like jade, of coming from the quarries in a workable state and slowly hardening on contact with the air.

Supetar is one of the best places in Dalmatia to recommend to a visitor who wants company, but not too much of it; who wants reasonable comfort, but not luxury; who has not too much money at his disposal, and who desires rest without solitude. It is clean and comfortable and picturesque. And Split is only an hour away by boat. Also, it makes a special and agreeable type of rakija out of green walnuts.

Supetar was the native town of the Petrinović family, some of whom emigrated to Chile and made there a stupendous fortune in the nitrate fields. In fact, the careers of some of the Yugoslav emigrants, like the Petrinovići or the Mihanovići, read like success stories of the nth degree. Here, too, they are buried; and their mausoleum is one of the most beautiful works of art in the world. This I can say with sincerity and conviction. It stands in the little cypress-planted graveyard, a few feet from the sea, and is the work of the great Yugoslav sculptor, Toma Rosandić.

Rosandić was himself a Dalmatian, though from the mountain land of the Lika. I knew him for years, and frequently visited his studio on the outskirts of Belgrade. When the war broke out, he, though an old man and crippled by arthritis, refused to live under the Germans and joined the partisans in the woods. Frankly, according to my friends, they were a little embarrassed to know what to do with him, but took the greatest care of his life and comfort, as far as such a word can be used for the conditions of guerilla warfare. For such artists are rare. But he lived, a free man and a great artist, and I saw him again after the war in his Belgrade studio.

Every part of this marvellous tomb is a work of art filled with piety and poetic truth. From the mourning angel, with wings folded over bent back and bowed head, on the top of the building, down to the corbels and brackets, every detail is perfect. The mausoleum itself is of white Brač stone, while the angel and the gates are of bronze.

The angel mourns, yet it is not the mourning of despair, while the figure of St Michael calls those within to a glorious resurrection. There is the pity and the compassion of death, without its terror and without its fear. The dead are waiting too, but they wait in hope and without suspense.

The bronze gates are the most lovely things of their kind that I have ever seen. On them the legions of good strive for the souls of the dead with the hosts of evil, but in their triumphant trumpets one sees ultimate victory.

To my mind it is a far greater work than the more famous Račić mausoleum by Ivan Meštrović at Cavtat. Here there is none of the tortured striving that mars Meštrović's work. Yet it is odious to make such comparisons. For Meštrović is essentially epic. The spirit of the Yugoslav epics, which he has so perfectly translated into stone, fills his work with vigour, force and heroism. Looking at it, one hears the sound of trumpets and of warriors shouting for battle. Rosandić is lyric. His sculpture is pure lyrical form and almost sensual beauty that makes one look and look again. The trumpets sounding here are the trumpets of the resurrection calling to eternal life; Meštrović would have made them the trumpets of the judgement. In Rosandić's work are all the tones of the orchestra, including the soft wail of the violins and the delicate filigree of the woodwind. One leaves Meštrović's mausoleum almost stunned; one leaves Rosandić's with a feeling of compassionate exaltation.

I have to admit that all my journeys to Vis were before the war. I say this designedly, for Vis during the war was a partisan head-quarters where the final offensives were planned, and there was a British supply mission there. The island was also bombed. I have been told that the vineyards were damaged, but that in the intervening years the damage has been made good.

This was not the first time that Vis has served as an Adriatic base. During the Continental System of Napoleon, the British seized Vis and Korčula and made them centres for the export of British goods to Central Europe and Germany via Bosnia and Croatia. The islands grew rich under this smugglers' regime and doubled in population. In 1811 the French Admiral Dubor-dieu attempted to drive the British from Vis, but was thoroughly defeated by a smaller British force under Hoste. A British grave-yard preserves the memory of this. We held the island until 1815, when it was handed over to Austria.

That was but one of many naval battles fought near Vis, the 'Adriatic Gibraltar', from the times of the Syracusans onwards. But that which most impressed the people was Tegetthoff's great victory in 1866. During the Italian occupation of 1918–21 the Italians in their usual manner took away the Lion of Vis which commemorated their defeat, but this piece of stone was merely a symbol and the memory remains.

It was a combination of curiosity and gluttony that led me to Vis. For the wines of Vis are as famous today throughout Yugo-slavia as they were throughout the polite world in classical times. 'In Lissa (Vis), an island of the Adriatic,' says Agatharchis, 'there grows a wine which, compared with any other, exceeds it in goodness.'

That, of course, was long before phylloxera days, but the heat and stones of Vis have even tamed the American vine to excellence. Indeed, on the tiny island of Biševo, opposite the village of Komiža on Vis, the old vines still exist. It was the only place in Dalmatia, perhaps in Europe, where the dreaded plague did not come. But its small production is scarcely enough to satisfy both islanders and connoisseurs.

It is strange that the phylloxera should ever have reached Vis. For it is the most distant of the Adriatic islands, far out in a sea that has long changed from shore-green to deep Adria blue. From the shore, it can only rarely be seen from great heights, such as Klis.

Biševo is even farther and even smaller. It has a Blue Grotto, rivalling Capri, which can be reached by fishing-boat. It is a lovely haunt of the sea-nymphs, while a little way away is the solitary rock needle of Jabuka, which is composed almost entirely of natural iron, so that it may well have been the loadstone-mountain that played such havoc with the mariners of Sinbad. I would have liked to see the Abbey church founded in the ninth century and to have tasted the Blue Grotto prošek from the old vines.

Komiža is first and foremostly a fishing village, and a large one. The air has an indefinable odour of fresh sardines, which is not unpleasant, and there are a number of canning factories, now co-operatives. The typical landscape has always a half-dozen nets or so drying in the sun. Those who are not engaged in fishing or in the factories or vineyards are either making or mending nets, and the place is as full of contented cats as Baška.

The rocky shores of Vis are good fishing-grounds, and those of Biševo and Sv. Andrija still better. But best of all are the rocky islets of Sušac and Pelargosa. Pelargosa today is uninhabited, save for an automatic lighthouse, if that may be classed as an inhabitant. At one time, when the fishing season opened, the harbour of Komiža presented a strange sight. As many as seventy fishing-vessels would line up across the harbour, and at a sign from the harbour-master would race the seventy odd kilometres to Pelargosa, rowing night and day, to get the choicest places for the coming season. It was no child's play, for the competition was severe and the boats heavy and clumsy. But the prizes were large, for whoever got the best position held it for the season. Today the ceremony no longer takes place, partly because of the use of motor vessels and partly because there are fewer competitors.

Komiža is a friendly place, and I soon found friends before the little kafana in the square known as the 'Battle of Vis,' after the victory of Tegetthoff, whose fleet was mainly manned by Dalmatians.

In its inception, the partisan movement had a distinctly moral tone. Perhaps that was necessary in an army where young men and girls shared equally in the dangers and discomforts of battle. Incidentally, they were profoundly shocked at the behaviour of their much-vaunted allies, the Red Army. But the war is receding into the background and is being forgotten save by those for whom it was the one great experience of their lives. The slightly priggish attitude of the first enthusiasts has been laughed into silence or forgotten. But some of the results remain. On the credit side, there is much less of the crude and indiscriminate swearing than there was before the war. On the debit side, there is the gradual disappearance of many of the old kafana names, which were considered 'not serious'. A perfectly stupid bit of reasoning; they were never intended to be serious. Thank goodness, the tide is turning and many of the old names are coming back.

These kafana names have the same flavour and tang as those of the old English pubs. They add a touch of colour and often remind one of the old traditions of their native place; witness the 'Battle of Vis'. But mostly they figure the host's name or nickname or are taken from the common incidents of the countryside, and are sometimes illustrated by vigorously painted frescoes on the outer wall or by a hanging sign. Belgrade has some of the best examples; the most famous centres of the local gourmets have fanciful names: 'At the Sign of the Three Hats', 'The Three Leaves of Tobacco', &c. I cannot refrain from quoting two of the best, both, alas, no longer existing. One was in Negotin and was called 'At the Sign of the Giraffe – an extraeuropean animal'; and the other was in a Belgrade side street. It was called 'The Seven Schwabes' (Germans). Its sign showed a rabbit holding back at spear's point seven terrified *landsknecht*.

But it was not the partisans who closed this last one. It closed, discreetly, during the German occupation.

However, we must return to Komiža. It has few antiquities, but some of interest. The main church of the town bears the curious title of 'Our Lady of the Pirates'. It contains a wonder-working picture of the Virgin which was once stolen by pirates. But every time they attempted to row past the point of the harbour, the power of the picture held them back, until at last they threw it into the sea and were free to go. Was the miracle invented to give credence to the name, or the name chosen to give credence to the miracle? It would be interesting to know. For in the original Croat it appears that Our Lady herself was the pirate!

Another church in the town has a more explicable miracle, in the form of a complicated mechanism invented by an ingenious priest for revealing and elevating the Sacrament without human aid, but now everyone in Komiža knows the secret, and it only amazes the country-women who come to see it on the rare occasions when it is still used. In this church there was once a relic still more wonderful to the faithful: the head of Jesus Christ Himself! But

The harbour of Hvar

there is a limit to credulity. This relic has been suppressed for many years.

But churches do not appeal to all. Komiža has another most interesting sight that has no connexion with miracles. The rocky coasts are full of lobsters and strange crabs. These fetch high prices in Zagreb, Belgrade and the Adriatic resorts. While awaiting shipment they are kept in a huge concrete basin, roofed over with boards, so that it is always cool and dark, like the sea caves that these creatures love. One circulates in this murky grot in a little boat, picking out enormous lobsters, crayfish or spider-crabs with a net, while the 'guardian-dogs' race frantically up and down the planks a foot or so above one's head, filling the air with clangour.

Hvar, close by, is one of the most attractive of the Dalmatian islands. It was a Greek settlement, though its name does not come, as I long thought, from 'pharos', a lighthouse, but from the fact that it was a colony of the men of Paros. In these islands from Hvar southwards, the historical background subtly changes. Venice is still in the centre of the stage, but other actors have come more prominently on the scene. At one time or another they all formed part of the Serbian Empire of the Nemanjas, and the Turk, whether as corsair or overlord, becomes ever more important. On the southernmost island, Lastovo, until the last war an Italian enclave, the principal church still has a sculptured head of Stefan Dečanski. Also many of them were within the borders of the Republic of Ragusa (Dubrovnik), whose influence is henceforth even more important than that of Venice.

This is particularly true of Hvar, where the famous corsair Uluz Ali burnt the city of Hvar in 1571 and made the inhabitants build up their lives again almost from scratch. Thus the main square of Hvar, one of the most beautiful in all Dalmatia, is largely surrounded by hollow shells of palaces which the inhabitants were not rich enough to rebuild after this disaster. The huge double fortress on the hill behind the city is of a later age; Spanish and Napoleonic.

Perhaps the most interesting building on Hvar was unaccountably overlooked by T. G. Jackson in his monumental work on the architecture of Dalmatia. This is the seventeenth-century (1612) theatre, the oldest in Yugoslavia. Today Hvar is a small place, and the theatre is only occasionally used for special presentations at the height of the tourist season. But it is pleasant to conjecture whether this little theatre was the cause or the effect of the short-lived but brilliant efflorescence of Slav literature in Hvar in the seventeenth and eighteenth centuries. The city then became, after Dubrovnik of course, the centre of Slav letters in the Adriatic. Most of the Hvar writers are somewhat dull and prosy to read at the present day, but the works of Hektorović, who wrote charming idylls on the lives of the fishermen of Hvar, are still fresh and interesting.

Hvar has good hotels and one of the finest beaches in all Dalmatia. For those who like more secluded spots, the chain of little islands that almost close the harbour entrance are ideal spots for a picnic. But one must take precautions and go well prepared, for though they are perfect for bathing or fishing, especially gun-fishing, they are both waterless and shadeless. For this reason they are known as Pakleni Otoci – 'The Islands of Hell'.

I have visited Hvar many times, but perhaps the most interesting occasion was once when I arrived unexpectedly and found the hotels full. An enterprising municipal official – they are very good at this – got me a room in the house of a local fisherman near the market. It was one of my pleasantest evenings. The local prošek is famous and the table-wine good. I spent hours discussing fishing with my host, and that night slept in the cool stone guest-room of his house, where the walls were fearsomely decorated with shells of enormous lobsters and the spiky-tailed king crabs of the Adriatic.

From the other side of the island one can see Biokovo and, nestling beneath it, Makarska. It is one of the most delightful spots on the coast for a pleasant holiday. Though badly damaged in the war, the ravages have been repaired. In any case, Makarska was never especially noted for its antiquities. But it has one of the best beaches in Dalmatia, and its situation, at the foot of the towering Biokovo, is magnificent.

Korčula, the 'Black Korkyra' of the Greeks, is ancient, though not as ancient as the famed Antenor inscription would have one believe. This states that Korčula arose out of the ashes of burning Troy, but it is well known that it was composed in the sixteenth century.

Korčula also has a cathedral. It is not, perhaps, so beautiful as those of Šibenik or Trogir, but it is extraordinarily interesting. In general design it is simply a large-scale Dalmatian church, but it has been decorated with stone carvings in the most perfect taste that give a curious sense of appliqué work; especially if one compares the elaborate façade with the severe simplicity of the back and sides. On each side of the main portal, representing once again the entry into Paradise, are Adam and Eve, on this occasion not so discreet, as they are both squatting in what I believe is known as the 'frog-position'. On the elaborate cornice are strange beasts in stone, including the famous elephants, which, however, are so conventionally carved that it is not easy to recognize them. There has been a lot of controversy about these beasts. Probably they were wrought to the designs of South Italian masters, who in turn had copied them from the Saracens. It would be a fascinating idea to connect them with Marco Polo, the most famous son of the island, and his stories of the East, which many believed for so long to have been mere traveller's tales, but there is unfortunately no evidence to allow one to do so. Poor Marco Millions! Once he set out on his travels he never saw Korčula again.

My last visit was, unfortunately, at the wrong time to see the knightly games of the Moreška, which take place on the patronal feast of St Theodore on June 29th each year. Their origin is uncertain; tradition assigns it to the brief period of Genoese rule between 1100 and 1129. The name means 'Moorish', and the subject is a struggle between the Moors and Ottomans. The black King Moro, with his followers dressed in black, in parody of Moorish dress, snatches from the Ottoman Sultan Osman his betrothed Bula (this word in Serb still means a veiled Turkish woman). Their followers fight, and then they themselves fight in single combat, Bula frantically intervening to save her beloved. With the final victory of Osman, the lovers are again united. The dances are rapid and rhythmical, requiring much skill and long training. In the fight scenes a novice might well receive a nasty blow. They fight each other with two swords, striking and parrying with extraordinary skill and precision; and there are no feigned blows. It is an interesting and exciting performance, well worth seeing.

Opposite Korčula, the long, narrow peninsula of Pelješac reaches out to sea, leaving only a narrow channel for the southward-bound steamers. On it are some of the most charming smaller seaside resorts of Dalmatia; Viganj, Kučište and Orebić. The people around here are an interesting ethnographical problem; those around Viganj are known locally as Farauni, otherwise Pharaohs, and their three villages are named Viganj (bellows), Nadkovan (anvil) and Kovaćevici (smiths). Surely this means a gipsy settlement which has forgotten its origin? For the smith's in the Balkans is a gipsy's trade, and even now, in England and elsewhere, the gipsies are sometimes known as Pharaohs.

From now on our old friend and travelling companion, Fortis, begins to desert us. For we are approaching the territory of the former Republic of Dubrovnik (Ragusa), which was an independent state in Fortis' time and not under Venetian control. Pelješac was a part of its territory, and Fortis did not cross the frontier.

In the deep-water channel behind Pelješac lies the estuary of the Neretva. It is little known to tourists, even though it no longer deserves its pre-war reputation for malaria. Though it has a certain melancholy beauty of its own, it is not cheerful. Its complicated creeks and marshes were the home of the Neretljani (Narentines), the most ferocious pirates of the earlier ages – from the days of Rome until the Turkish conquest. Even then a large number of them refused to submit to the Turks, and under the Vlatković family moved to the northern coast where they became the ancestors of the brave but bloodthirsty Uskoks. Incidentally, they remained pagan long after the conversion of the other Slavs.

The course of the river winds through desolate marshy lagoons and salt-marshes. In these lagoons breed the pelicans. Or so say the guide-books. I have never been lucky enough to see one here, though I have seen them on the Lake of Skadar. A wonderful bird is the pelican!

Of Metković, the less said the better. It lies between two worlds. There is no more good Dalmatian wine and as yet no good Bosnian coffee.

CHAPTER VIII

City of the Argosies: Dubrovnik

Glories of the argosies – A thousand years of freedom – Last days with Ivo Saraka – Nobles and plebs – Spanish ties – The Armada and Queen Elizabeth – A mediaeval welfare state – Yugoslav mediaeval writers – The mausoleum at Cavtat.

The argosies no longer enter the ancient harbour of Dubrovnik. Its cool waters, overlooked by a huge terraced café, are now given over to yachts and an occasional fishing-boat. The modern steamships, that have neither their romance nor their rich freights, come to Gruž, outside the city walls.

The last of the great argosies was sold after the earthquake that almost destroyed the city in 1667. After that time Dubrovnik had only smaller vessels, and even the last of these was confiscated by, of all people, the English during the Napoleonic wars. That was in November 1813, when the ancient republic was in its death-throes. It had been abolished a few years before by Marshal Marmont, but a few nobles tried, bravely but unsuccessfully, to revive it.

'Argosy', a word that English poets have transfigured to mean a treasure galleon, laden with wealth, adventure and romance, means nothing more than 'a ship of Ragusa' (Dubrovnik).

For centuries, and especially in Renaissance times, the Ragusans were the great merchant-adventurers of their day. Though small and weak when compared with the apparently boundless resources of Venice – a census, the first taken in 1673, shortly after the earthquake, gave only just over 30,000 souls for the whole territory of the republic – Dubrovnik was her great rival in the Adriatic and Levant trade, and even surpassed her in trade with the Ottoman Empire. She owed her wealth and position to the bravery and daring of her merchants and to the persuasive skill of her diplomats, without which so small a state could never have

Dubrovnik

left its mark on history. Her sailors and galleys were ever in demand; later nominal overlords demanded from Dubrovnik only that some of her ships should join their fleets in time of war. Thus Dubrovnik often came into conflict with the growing sea-power of the English, especially when employed by Philip of Spain in the English and Dutch wars of the sixteenth century. A Dubrovnik contingent sailed with the Armada, and their superior seamanship enabled many to escape from that disaster. Dubrovnik nobles rose to high rank at the Spanish Court and some even became grandees. One of the most fascinating unproved theories of history concerns distant Fair Isle. It is known that a Dubrovnik vessel was wrecked on the island after the dispersal of the Armada. Today the well-known patterns of Fair Isle show a close resemblance to those of the Konavle, and the name of one of the leading Fair Isle families is very similar to that of the Dubrovnik shipmaster Mardešić.

Dubrovnik is not one of the most ancient cities of Dalmatia. It is first mentioned by Constantine Porphyrogenitos, who says it was founded after the sack of Epidauros by the Slavs in the seventh century. Epidauros, across the bay, is the modern Cavtat (from *civitas vetus* – i.e. the old city), and its Italian name is Ragusa Vecchia.

The refugees founded a settlement, Ragusa, on the present site of Dubrovnik, and for centuries preserved their Latin tongue and way of life against the encroachments of the Slavs. The present Stradun was then a marshy creek, on the opposite side of which a Slav settlement grew up. The two cities grew, but did not mingle. It is not until the end of the thirteenth century that one finds Slav names in the roll of the Ragusan nobility, and then mainly among the women. But the process was undoubtedly hastened by the enclosure of the two cities in a common system of fortifications in 1272. By the fifteenth century the slavization of the city was almost complete, though the 'Ragusan language' was still mainly spoken and the city was always known as Ragusa. After the disasters of 1667 the name Dubrovnik came into common use.

Dubrovnik was, in practice, a free and independent city for over eight centuries. But discretion and diplomacy usually demanded a nominal overlord, to whom either a small annual tribute was paid or a contribution of war-galleys promised, to ensure external peace and a free development of trade. The representative of this overlord never had any power within the city and usually dwelt outside its walls.

At first nominally a part of the Eastern Empire, Ragusa had little contact with Constantinople, and the Byzantine strategos usually lived in Zadar. In the ninth century, when the city was attacked by the Arabs, it defended itself for fifteen months without outside aid. About the year 1000 it was attacked by the Croats, but in alliance with the great Venetian Doge Pietro Orseolo it drove them off as well.

The noble families of Ragusa were merchants rather than warriors. War harmed their trade. They preferred to acquire lands by purchase and diplomacy and never extended their possessions beyond the nearby coast and islands. After the Croat invasion had been beaten back, Croat and later Serbian rulers treated the city as a sovereign state.

But Ragusa could not escape the curse of all mediaeval city-states. The extremely complicated constitution of the city and the rivalries between groups of nobles developed into faction wars.

To ensure internal peace a neutral podestà was called in from
Venice; but neither Venetian podestà nor later Ragusan Rector
had any real power. Never once was any foreigner allowed to
interfere in internal affairs. Podestà or Rector was, at best, an
arbitrator. The power always lay with the Council of Nobles, of
which the Minor Council was an executive instrument.

Meanwhile Venice and Ragus developed side by side, without
rivalry, for there was trade enough in the Levant for both. But
while Venice tended more and more to become a centralized and
military oligarchy, Ragusa developed towards a patrician
democracy. The Doge soon became a powerful figure; the
power of the Rector was gradually whittled away till finally he
was elected for a month only and, once that month had ended,
could not display the emblems of his former rank again until the
day of his death, when they were placed upon his coffin.

By the thirteenth century Dubrovnik was already signing
treaties as a sovereign state. In 1252 one was signed with the
Bulgarian Tsar Michael Asen. Her trade increased mightily and
her diplomatic power with it. She was soon on good terms with
the Serbian Empire of the Nemanjas. It is true that that uneasy
and ambitious dynasty tried, from time to time, to control Dubrovnik as they already controlled Kotor; but the city was never taken,
and the most powerful of the Nemanjas, Stefan Dušan the Mighty,
confirmed their friendship. It was a delegation of Dubrovnik
nobles that had reconciled him to his aged father, Stefan Dečanski,
with whom he had quarrelled, and the great tsar himself was
welcomed to Dubrovnik and addressed the nobles in the Hall of
the Great Council.

On the tiny island of Lastovo there is a sculpture of Stefan
Dečanski, cheek by jowl with the ruined summer palaces of the
Dubrovnik nobles.

It was after the death of Dušan and the disintegration of the
Serbian Empire that the diplomatic genius of Dubrovnik scored
its most signal success. It was soon evident to the Council that
the petty and divided states of Macedonia and Serbia were no
match for the rising military power of the Turks. Their judgement was soon confirmed by the battle of Kosovo, where the
Serbo-Bosnian coalition was signally defeated by the sultan. That

was the death-blow, though wealthy Serb states continued to live, on Turkish sufference, in a sort of twilight independence for another seventy years. The last Serbian ruler to enter Dubrovnik was the Despot George Branković, and he came as a suppliant, pursued by the vengeance of Murad II. Dubrovnik was ordered to hand him over. The Council refused, with the famous reply:

'We men of Dubrovnik have nothing but our faith and, by our faith, we would have behaved towards you in the same manner had you come hither.'

But private faith went hand in hand with public diplomacy. It was clear that the power of the Serbs was broken, so the nobles offered the overlordship of the city to the distant king of Hungary, and at almost the same time negotiated a trade agreement with the Turks, which saved the city after the final overthrow of the Christian power in the Balkans.

I saw that treaty in the house of Ivo Saraka a little before the war. His ancestors had been among those who signed it. Šjor Ivo was then a very old man. With him disappeared almost the last of the direct line of the old Dubrovnik nobles, the vlastela.

Most of the noble families have died out, as if they realized that they were no longer in place in this modern striving world and preferred to leave behind them a fragrant and romantic memory rather than a picture of decadence and decay. The Sorgos are represented only by collateral branches of another name. The Restis are no more. The Ranjinas, whose poems and plays are part of the great heritage of Yugoslav literature, can now be traced only in their works or on the carved coat-of-arms over the doors of their one-time palace. The Ohumučevići, who made most of their fortune in Spain, have also gone. A slab in the Dominican monastery records that a member of their family was an admiral in the Spanish Armada whose seamanship in English waters astonished the Spaniards and so annoyed Queen Elizabeth that she wrote furious letters to the Ottoman sultan demanding that he punish the presumptuous city. The Gondola-Gundulić – almost every Ragusan family had both a Slav and a Latin name – have also died out, though the works of Ivan Gundulić are still read and his statue decorates the public square. Only the Bonas, the Gozze-Gučetići, the Kabogas and one or two others still survive. But they, too, are dying out, and that will be the end.

I still recall that last conversation with Ivo Saraka. We might
have been sitting in a Rembrandt picture, save that the faces in
the lamplight – Šjor Ivo always refused to have electric light –
were of that clear-cut, medallion type characteristic of the south,
not the victorious pagan south of Tintoretto or Correggio, but
the ascetic south of El Greco, who was trained by a Dalmatian.
The face of my companion opposite was deeply etched in shadow,
every line and wrinkle clearly outlined, while naked cupids and
voluptuous nymphs showed uncertainly around him, when the
wick burned higher, from a painted cabinet behind. He, an
everyday citizen of Dubrovnik, spoke with a strange mixture of
deference and familiarity. Saraka, at the other end of the table,
might have been carved in stone, save for the movement of his
lips and the occasional flash of his eyes. Now and again he put his
hand to his head. His white expanse of forehead and great hooked
nose made him seem like an amiable but aristocratic vulture.

He spoke of the past of Dubrovnik and the pride of her nobles,
in a broad Ragusan dialect in which the basic Slav was freely
mingled with Latin and Italian. His memory was prodigious. I
asked him about the Feast of Sv. Vlaho, the patron saint of the
republic.

'It served to hold the republic together. Once a year at least
the people saw the city and its power. We nobles encouraged it.
We were a close community and kept the rites of Catholicism
very strictly. We even maintained a sort of unofficial literary
censorship among ourselves. Once, when the Dutch Ambassador
was here he refused to kneel to the Host. "I do not believe," he
said, "that that is really the body of Christ." "And do you think
we believe?" answered a noble. "But we kneel just the same – for
the sake of the people." And the Ambassador knelt. No – we
were all humanists, platonists. We worshipped Plato – and we
lived by Petrarch.

'Only by keeping the forms and ceremonies strictly could we
survive; and by maintaining the power of the nobles. Think of
us for a minute: a tiny republic, with Venice and the Emperor
on the one side, and the Serbs and afterwards the Turks on the
other. Do you see that scroll?' and he pointed to a document in

Arabic script on the wall. 'That is the original treaty with the sultan for trading rights, before the Turks entered Europe – in the fourteenth century. That scroll there is the sultan's toghrul. So, when they came, we were not a country to be conquered, but an allied state. We knew they would come; and we knew they would win. Our secret service was the best in the world.'

This treaty of 1365 with Sultan Murad gave Dubrovnik freedom of trade within the confines of the Ottoman Empire. As that Empire extended over all the Balkans and up to the gates of Vienna, the merchants of Dubrovnik were to be found in all its greater cities. They had their own quarters in Belgrade, Sofia, Skopje, Constantinople. They controlled the mines of Novo Brdo, the textiles of Sofia, the salt monopoly of Ston. Their trade increased by leaps and bounds. By 1462 there were 7,000,000 ducats in the city treasury.

The prosperity of the Ottoman Empire meant the prosperity of Dubrovnik. But there was a price to be paid. Every year a deputation of nobles left for Istanbul with an annual tribute to which, according to Ottoman custom, had to be added rich gifts for dragomen and viziers. There were always rival and envious traders who cast greedy eyes at Dubrovnik's practical monopoly of the internal carrying trade. But the annual tribute was delivered almost in a triumphal procession, and the Sublime Porte treated the city as a sovereign and independent state.

This maze of diplomacy had placed Dubrovnik in a privileged position. But at the same time it was an anomalous one. In the West she was regarded as the protector of the Catholic Church in the Balkans, and the Porte recognized this right, at least implicitly. So, at the same time, Dubrovnik was allied with His Most Catholic Majesty of Spain, and Dubrovnik nobles became Spanish grandees, though it is hard to recognize such names as Mažibradić or Skočibuha in their Iberian forms. The ships of Dubrovnik, by one alliance, had to take part in many naval expeditions against the Moslems; by the other they must keep peace with the Porte. This double face was successfully maintained, but at considerable cost behind closed doors.

Besides, Venice, once almost an elder brother to the infant republic, had now become her most embittered foe and rival.

Venetian intrigue tried to turn the Pope against Dubrovnik, but the Pope realized the difficulties of the position and would take no action.

As long as the Ottoman Empire remained vigorous and expanding, the prosperity of Dubrovnik was assured. The rule of the Ottomans, though harsh and infidel, was at least as just as that of the feudal monarchies they had displaced. But when the long decline of the Empire set in, with all its accompanying unrest, corruption and anarchy, the decline of Dubrovnik set in also. That decline was first heralded by a series of natural calamities. In 1520 the city was shattered by an earthquake and in 1527 there was a serious visitation of the plague. Yet the republic was still strong enough to beat off an attack by the dreaded pirates of Africa and to maintain for another century her monopoly of the carrying trade of the Balkans.

The decisive blow came on Easter Day, 1667. A terrific earthquake shook the city. Even the walls were broken. More than two-thirds of the inhabitants perished. Bands of brigands invaded the city to finish what the earthquake had begun. A noble, Nikola Bona, mustered those patricians remaining alive and guarded the ruins of the Treasury in person. Venice waited on the side-lines, hoping that famine and disaster would force the republic to become her vassal. There were serious consultations in the depleted Major Council about abandoning the site of the city altogether and rebuilding the republic elsewhere. These faint-hearted proposals were largely defeated by the patriotism of two nobles, Nikola Bona and Marojica Kaboga.

New blood had to be introduced to repair the devastation. More and more Slav names are to be found from now onwards in the roll of the nobles. More and more the common people of the city became Slav in blood and language. More and more the new-comers clamoured for a share in the government from which, at first, they were rigorously excluded.

Not only among the people had the ravages of the earthquake to be repaired. The greater part of the city had to be rebuilt. Many of the most famous buildings were destroyed, including the Gospa, the original cathedral, built partly by the grateful donations of King Richard Coeur de Lion. Few of the ancient buildings survived the shocks; of them the most important were the two monasteries, Dominican and Franciscan, the Customs House, and a great part of the Rector's Palace. The main line of the ancient walls remained, though damaged, and one or two of the ancient monuments, such as the famous fountain of Onofrio della Cava and the Orlando Column, the rallying point of the republic, on which its standard was displayed on feast days. Most of the ordinary dwelling-houses were destroyed, and the regulations for rebuilding the city enacted that all new ones must be of stone and conform to a certain type – one of the earliest and most successful examples of town-planning.

Indeed, it is remarkable how modern this little group of governing nobles was. A system of state medical assistance was decreed in 1301, a public apothecary (his shop and many of his utensils still exist to amuse the curious visitor) in 1318, a hospital for the poor in 1347, a hostel for foreign visitors in 1423 and a foundling hospital in 1432. Torture as a legal procedure was abolished at the end of the seventeenth century. The inquisition never set foot in the city, and there is no example in its history of any person being burnt alive. The excesses of the slave trade were modified in 1312 and the trade itself abolished in 1416. It is only necessary to compare these dates with parallel ones among the neighbouring Turks and Venetians, or even contemporary France and England, to see how much this tiny republic was ahead of its times.

It was shortly after the great earthquake, when the Treasury was depleted for the rebuilding of the city, that Dubrovnik was called upon to face another crisis. The Turkish Grand Vizier, Kara Mustafa, obsessed with his dream of conquering Vienna, demanded increased tribute. But the Treasury could not meet the demand, and the pasha of Bosnia was ordered to make war on the republic. The Council of Nobles sat long, debating how to pacify the pasha and placate the extortionate vizier. Volunteers were called for, to parley with them. Such a mission promised almost certain death.

Finally four nobles offered to go; they were Marojica Gozze-Gučetić and Nikola Bona to approach the pasha, Marojica Kaboga and Djura Buć to appease the vizier. Their orders have been preserved in the records of the republic. They ran:

'To violence you will reply by renunciation and sacrifice; promise nothing, give nothing, suffer everything. The Republic is watching you. Over there you will meet a glorious death, but here will be a free land. In case of difficulty, postpone. Be of one accord and reply that we are free men, that this is tyranny and that God will judge them.'

The two envoys to Istanbul were at once thrown into prison, whence they did not emerge till the arrival of the tribute caravan the following year. Those who went to the Bosnian pasha met a worse fate. The Ottoman armies had been sent to the Danube against the Russians, and the pasha with them. The two envoys followed. There, on the low, swampy plains around Silistria, Bona died of a fever, denied even the consolations of his religion. Gučetić continued to hold out. It was not until the Ottoman army was defeated before the walls of Vienna, and the disgraced Kara Mustafa sentenced to the bow-string, that he was allowed to return. The usual figure of the tribute was maintained.

There is a table to the memory of Bona in the Hall of the Minor Council. It is the only memorial to an individual patrician in the whole city. It describes him as 'a senator of exceptional wisdom and immortal fame'.

Venice, too, tried to prey upon the weakened republic. However the diplomats of Dubrovnik at the Peace of Požarevac managed to ensure that two tiny Turkish enclaves – at Klek and Sutorina – separated the Adriatic possessions of the two republics. But her great days were over. She continued, indeed, to trade with the Ottoman Empire for another century, but it was a weakened city, divided by faction, that had to face Napoleon's marshals in 1806. On New Year's Day, 1808, Marmont, ironically created Duc de Raguse, took his seat beside the last of the Rectors, Sabo Georgić, and declared that the ancient republic had ceased to exist.

A last flicker of independence blazed up for a moment in 1813 when the Austrian General Milutinović attacked the city, then under French occupation. A group of nobles hoisted the ancient standard of the republic. But their movement was soon suppressed. It was then, incidentally, that the English confiscated the last ships of Dubrovnik. But by then they belonged no longer to the city of the argosies.

Thenceforward Dubrovnik lived the stagnant and somnolent life of a small and distant Austrian provincial town, and only awoke once more at the liberation of 1918.

Though the last of the argosies had been sold after the great earthquake and the trade and wealth of Dubrovnik began visibly to decline, the sixteenth and seventeenth centuries were a time of artistic renaissance. The influence of contemporary Italian literature was strong, and many Dubrovnik writers wrote also in that language and took a high place in Italian letters. Dante and Petrarch found many admirers and imitators. Life was easy and carefree, the bonds of the Church were relaxed. Masquerades, pastorals and comedies took the place of the liturgies and church services of earlier times.

The luxury of the patricians was extreme; in 1521 Marin Georgić brought Titian himself from Italy to paint the walls of his palace at Gruž, and Vlaho Sorkočević produced pastorals in the great hall of his palace as early as 1549.

This love of the theatre has continued to the present day, and the spectacles of recent Dubrovnik festivals have been staged in much the same places and in much the same conditions as in the sixteenth and seventeenth centuries.

One of the Dubrovnik playwrights still holds the stage, at least in his native city. He is Marin Držić (1510–67). He gives a true picture of the renaissance in Dubrovnik when, to use his own phrase, the city had 'its belly full of wine to the throat'. In his comedies he created a number of excellent types from Ragusan society, and showed himself rich in experience of men and women, from which he himself was never able to profit. Through his comedies dart merry lovers, old people ridiculous in their passions, unfaithful wives, spendthrifts, courtesans, venal servants, misers, thick-headed husbands and naïve peasants. He was a true precursor of Molière, who might easily have uttered his sarcastic remark: 'Without a penny one cannot even say a prayer.'

The seventeenth century, after the great earthquake, was for Dubrovnik a period of political and commercial decline, but of literary exuberance. The number of poets and writers in Slav was then legion. More emphasis was then laid upon Slav themes, and the marked Italian influence of the previous century is less noticeable. It is also the great period of Dubrovnik latinity – the last, indeed, in which Yugoslav writers of importance used that tongue, culminating in the work of the Jesuit Roger Bošković (1711–87), whose *Theoria Philosophiae naturalis*, published in 1758, became world famous.

I have left little space to speak of all the pleasant places around Dubrovnik where something of the aristocratic spirit of the old republic seems to linger. But no one should forget the Dubrovačka Rijeka, where the Ombla, in the magical manner of karst rivers, springs full grown out of the mountain-side to form a wide stream where great ships may lie at anchor. This place was chosen by the nobles of Dubrovnik for their summer palaces, of which some remain. They had taste and a sense of beauty.

Nor should Ston, where there is an ancient church that shows the translation from Byzantine to early Romanesque, be forgotten. It has also excellent oysters.

Nor should you forget Mljet of the mongooses.

Despite the pundits, I still agree with the Reverend Abbot Ignjat Djurdjević of the Congregatio Melitensis who wrote in 1730 of St Paul's shipwreck. To a lay eye, everything suits his theory. Paul's road to Rome would surely have lain up the Adriatic when approached from the stormy south. It was called Melita in Paul's time. Also it had plenty of snakes; the mongooses are a recent importation for that very reason. No, the old abbot had good grounds.

And lastly Cavtat, the ancient Epidauros, which many claim to be the mother of Dubrovnik. In those early times it was the most important city between the Neretva and the Boka. In the times of the flowering of the Dubrovnik Republic it was bought by Dubrovnik and used as a sort of state port when Serb or Bosnian rulers visited the city.

The great pride of Cavtat, however, is the Račić mausoleum, by Ivan Meštrović. It is a marvellously impressive monument, simple and severe at first sight, with a certain epic grandeur, though not very large. The bronze doors, between two lovely and serene caryatids, depict the four Slavonic apostles or saints: Cyril, Methodius, Gregory and Sava. Inside, the ceiling is wonderfully designed, with angels' heads gazing downwards in mathematical precision at a mosaic pavement of the four evan-gelists with their attendant beasts. A figure of St Rok, with his ever-faithful dog at his feet, is superb.

Indeed, superb and austere are the words that come to mind in describing it. Yet to me it is curiously inhuman, the product of an intelligence that has sensed rather than experienced beauty. Here Meštrović has more harmony than in his sculptures, say, at Split, but he has lost something of his force, and, in so doing, something of his peculiar attraction. Death does not seem to mean so much to him as life; here it is a state of cold and static appre-hension, not, as in the Rosandić mausoleum at Brač, an awesome yet gentle mystery and hope. No one can come away from this tomb unimpressed. Yet, if I had the choice, I would rather lie in Brač.

CHAPTER IX

'First the Men of Perast':
The Boka Kotorska

The most ancient seamen's guild – Mediaeval religious tolerance – Watchers of the fjord – The Isle of the Dead – Links with the Nemanjas – Spaniards and Jews – Budva – Sv. Stefan – The deserted village – Ulcinj, city of the corsairs.

'First the men of Perast, then the men of Zlarin, then the men of Bakar, and then the rest.'

Perast is in the Boka, the home of the most ancient confraternity of the sea. The rules of the Guild of Boka Sailors (Bokeljska Mornarica) far outdate the ancient Laws of Oleron. Only Rhodes has a prior, if doubtful, claim. The Statute was revised in 1463, which is the date of the document usually shown to visitors, but the records of the Guild go back to 809, when the patronage was transferred from St Nicholas, patron of all sailors, to Sv. Trifun, patron saint of Kotor. Perhaps even earlier.

For the sailors of the Boka have always been accounted the finest in Dalmatia. Not only Kotor itself, but Prčanj, Dobrota, Perast and the other cities of the Boka were famous for their daring and skilful navigators. When the land behind the mountains ceased to be Slav and became Turk, this reputation declined, but their skill and daring continued to be used in the service of other nations. The place of honour on the ships of the Venetian admirals was reserved for the navigators of Perast who led their ships at Lepanto. Later, Peter the Great, though he learnt his shipbuilding and navigation in Holland and in England, enrolled his sailors from the Boka. The staff of the first great Russian admiral, Zmajević, is still preserved in the cathedral of Sv. Trifun. A few of the original families who were members of the Guild still exist in Kotor, and I notice in a history of the Guild dated 1899 – i.e.

under Austrian rule – that the Admiral of the Mornarica, Count Antun Trifun Luković, was then living in Cardiff.

The Boka for a moment became the centre of interest during the last war, when an attempt was made to embark there the British Legation convoy, composed of the diplomatic staff and most of the British, as well as a good many of the Allied, residents in Yugoslavia at that time. The attempt failed, and many persons have, in consequence, bitter memories of the Boka. For myself, I tried to find another way, overland. But I failed, too, and probably fared worse. But my memories of the Boka remain unimpaired.

I always enter the Boka with a lightening of heart. Not only is its natural beauty so striking as to be always new and always ready to reveal some fresh facet of awe-inspiring majesty, but the character of the people is subtly different from that of the inhabitants of northern Dalmatia. Perhaps the sea has given them a wider outlook, or perhaps the solemn grandeur of their mountain fjord. Whatever the reason, the people of the Boka are of mixed creeds, the majority Orthodox, with Catholics in some of the cities. But they live together in broad-minded tolerance. Earlier, especially in the times of Tvrtko of Bosnia's overlordship, there were also a number of Bogumils, and unique instances are known in the Boka history of co-operation between prelates of all three creeds. On one such occasion a Bogumil religious leader joined with the Catholic bishops in anathematizing a member of his flock who had robbed a Catholic church. And a little south of the Boka itself, at Sutomore, there is a church with two altars where the rival services are solemnized alternately and without friction! The people of the Boka are more open-hearted, simple and hospitable. Their pride is the sea, and their patriotism wide and all-embracing.

The watchers of the fjord are the fortresses of Oštro and Mamula. Then you enter the outer bay, about 15 miles long, and thence through the Verige, a narrow strait once closed by chain-booms, into the inner bay, as large as the outer, where is Kotor itself, Perast, Risan and many other famous cities. The whole is encircled by mountains, rising to 6,000 or 7,000 feet from the water's edge. Those on the left are the Krivošije, snow-capped for half the year, whose sturdy highlanders withstood the Austrians and

defied the whole might of the Empire for more than a decade.
On the right is Lovćen.

Once through the Verige, the immensity of the Boka is almost
frightening. The mountains press menacingly forward to the
narrow strip of cultivated land where the cities stand, as if threaten-
ing to push them and their vineyards and olive-groves into the
still, dark waters of the inner gulf. In ancient times they actually
did so, for ancient Risan (Rhizon), the capital of the Illyrians and
seat of that most ferocious enemy of Rome, Queen Teuta, was
overwhelmed by a landslide. Traces of its masonry may still be
seen on clear days far down under the water.

Facing Perast are the twin islands of St George and the Gospa
od Škrpelja, each with its church. The island of the Gospa is said
to have been built artificially of stone by the Perastines in fulfilment
of a vow. Certainly it was the graveyard of the city when it was at
the height of its power. The tall sentinel cypresses around the little
church and the black water – for the sun penetrates late into this
corner of the Boka – make it seem like an island in Lethe, and one
watches to catch sight of Charon setting out with his barque from
deserted Perast to ferry a few more souls to eternal forgetfulness.
No wonder Böcklin chose it for his 'Isle of the Dead'.

For Perast is now deserted. The beautiful renaissance palaces
are empty, and the great church seems still more desolate when
filled with the few fishermen who still live in the shadow of that
former glory. Ichabod!

Kotor itself is, however, still vigorous and progressive, for it
has now its natural hinterland, from which it was so long cut off
in Venetian and Austrian times by political barriers. Perhaps it
is the most impressive of the Boka cities, for immediately behind
it rises the tremendous mass of the Lovćen, the entry to the Black
Mountain itself, up whose precipitous sides you may see the hairpin
serpentines of the road to Cetinje. Half-way up the mountain-side
a white dot marks the gendarmerie station which was the former
frontier blockhouse. The people of Kotor say that the winter snows
cease at this point, as if fearing to pass the former boundary.

With Kotor and the cities of the Boka there is another subtle
change in the historical background. Venice does not become
important until the fifteenth century; before that the canvas is

Illyrian, Byzantine or Slav. Kotor, in particular, had especially close relations with her Slav neighbours. With an internal organization somewhat similar to that of Dubrovnik, Kotor, too, relied on trade and diplomacy. But her resources were not equal to her deserts, and her relations with her overlords were closer, though mainly cordial. She was the chief seaport of the Slav state of Zeta, the ancestor of Montenegro, even as later she was to become the main outlet for that theocratic marchland. She had particularly close relations with the Nemanjas. The Emperor Stefan Dušan refers to her as 'our most loyal, capital, and well-beloved and glorious city of Kotor', while earlier the greatest of the Nemanjas, Sv. Sava, made the Gulf of Kotor the centre of his Eparchia of Zeta at the time of his reorganization of the Serbian Orthodox Church. The bishop resided on the little island of Prevlaka, near present-day Tivat. Her relations with King Tvrtko of Bosnia, who regarded himself, with some reason, as the successor to the Nemanjas, were also very cordial.

After the fall of the Serbian power, when the Boka became for a time a Venetian lake, the Venetians, too, gave signal honour to Kotor. She was made the seat of the Grande Provveditore of the Province of Venetian Albania.

The market of Kotor is bright with the national costumes of the Montenegrins. They look strangely exotic under the frowning Venetian battlements, still decorated with the arms of the noble families. Some of these families are indeed noble, both by descent and by achievement. In the days when Kotor was the port of the Serbian Empire, it was Nikola Buć who was the famous chamberlain of Tsar Dušan, and it was a friar of Kotor, Vid the Franciscan, who built the church of High Dečani, perhaps the most beautiful in all Serbia.

The streets of Kotor are even narrower and more confusing than those of Split or Šibenik. One can spend a good half-hour trying to find the way to the cathedral of Sv. Trifun in a city really not very much bigger than a pocket handkerchief. It is a wonderful old church, dating in its present state from 1166, but built on an older foundation of 809. A gateway of the older church is still preserved in the sacristy, showing intricate Slavonic ornamentation somewhat similar to the Anglo-Saxon style.

But Kotor is hot, very hot, and somewhat airless. To bathe there is like bathing in a conservatory, and the water always seems like warm milk. For everyday pleasures I prefer the outer bay of the Boka, and more especially Hercegnovi, perhaps my favourite resort in all Dalmatia.

One of the most lovely tourist excursions in Yugoslavia is the Boka–Montenegro tour. The coaches start from Dubrovnik or Hercegnovi, go around the Boka by way of Risan and Perast to Kotor itself, and then up the serpentines of the Lovćen road to Cetinje. The view of the Boka from the summit of the pass is one of the most astounding in all Europe. Kotor itself is hidden, since it lies right under the slope of the mountain, but on the other hand one can see the whole magnificent stretch of the Boka and the mountains, often snow-capped, of the Krivošije. No one should miss it; it is worth several stars in any guidebook. Also, the Montenegrin chauffeurs have been weaned of their earlier habit of driving around these famous hairpin bends with one leg over the steering-wheel while using both hands to point out to the panic-stricken passengers the beauties through which they are passing. I have known several people who have taken this truly marvellous trip and could recall nothing of it afterwards; so terrified were they at this expertize that they could not take their eyes off the tremendous mountain slopes at the edge of the road. The trip usually returns by the Župa and Grbalj valleys and Budva.

For myself, I have taken the trip many times, and prefer to enter Montenegro by another and less-frequented way. That is by steamer to Ulcinj, the southernmost point of the Yugoslav Adriatic and almost on the Albanian frontier. This trip also passes Budva, but on the seaward side.

Hercegnovi was originally a fortress of Tvrtko, king of Bosnia, and later a Venetian and Spanish fortress, continually taken and re-taken in the Turkish wars. The whole episode of the Spanish incursions into these waters is a fascinating and romantic one, but it would take too long to tell it here. The little town, with its ominous fortress ruins glowering over the pleasant modern plage, makes a lovely sight as the ship leaves, and one that will be long remembered.

As the ship leaves the Boka, it cruises along the shores of the Luštica peninsula. This is a sparsely peopled district, a little pocket of primitivism between the Boka and Budva. Traces of the blood feud still linger in the customs of the people, and just before the war there was a formal reconciliation of two rival tribes, with ceremonies that have been forgotten elsewhere for more than a century. One of the villages of this district is made up of Orthodox Serbs, but all with Spanish names. I went there once, trying to discover their origins, but was unsuccessful as they knew nothing of their ancestors. Usually a Spanish name in the Balkans means a Jew, as the Balkan Jews are nearly all descendants of the Sephardi, driven out of Spain by Ferdinand and Isabella the Catholic, and have preserved not only their names but also their language. But this village did not seem to fit the bill. For one thing, they had forgotten their origins and their language, and save for their names were as Serb as their neighbours. Secondly, Jews seldom become peasants (with the notable exception of modern Israel), but rather traders and townspeople. Thirdly, they had no Jewish characteristics of appearance or gesture. I finally concluded that they must be descendants of the Spanish soldiers who once held Hercegnovi and who had been sent across the bay when the new masters took charge. But that is only a hypothesis.

Once out of the shelter of the Boka the ship turns southward. This coast was the step-child both of the Venetians and the Austrians. The only interest they took in it was to see that it did not belong to Montenegro. The extraordinary beauty and the quality of its bathing-beaches did not interest them. For there are no islands to shelter the coast, and the shallow sandy bays that are so splendid for bathers were worse than useless for harbours. Until far south, at Bar, there is no harbour for large ships. And the hinterland was Montenegro, so there was little trade. It was left to dream on for centuries in primitive neglect.

Since the liberation of 1918 the coast has been able to draw on the touristic resources of Yugoslavia and has gone ahead rapidly. Though exposed in winter to the force of the sea gales – farther south in Albania it becomes very harsh and dangerous; the Acroceraunian Cape had an exceedingly bad reputation in classical and mediaeval times – it is fresher and cooler in the long summer.

The express steamers which ply along the whole Adriatic coast usually end their trip at Ulcinj. There is also a frequent service from the Boka ports in smaller vessels. Personally, I find trips by these smaller ships more amusing, and usually travel as a deck-passenger. There is nothing pleasanter than to curl up on a coil of rope under the warm Dalmatian sun and watch the coast slip slowly by, in the intervals of dozing. Down to Kotor, one's companions are likely to be young excursionists with a sprinkling of peasants; after Kotor, more peasants and fewer excursionists, as the boats are the main regular communication. But they are good company and can tell one more about the coast and its towns and villages than a score of guide-books. Also the captain and the sailors on the smaller boats are friendly and communicative and – an important point for those who do not speak Serbo-Croat – likely to know English or some major European language.

When the sun begins to weaken, one or another group will almost always start a folk-song, and there is no better time to listen to them. If the sea is calm, it is more than likely they will begin to dance as well. But this depends on the cargo; the usual peasant dance – the kolo – requires plenty of room.

But the fresh sea air makes one hungry and the boats are often crowded. Catering facilities are apt to become exhausted or, at best, very limited. It is well to take some reserve with you.

After Miločer, the coast becomes steep and precipitous, with cliffs dropping hundreds of feet to the water's edge. On the hills behind are dotted tiny Orthodox monasteries, some of them of great age.

One of the most interesting of these is the monastery of Gradište near Petrovac. It has three churches dating by popular tradition to the twelfth century, but the frescoes were the work of Pop (priest) Strahinja and were painted in 1620. They have been considerably damaged by damp, but there is one unique portrait, more or less intact, that of a donkey carrying a cross, its head surrounded by a halo. Students of early Christian symbolism should find it interesting.

Once past the Boka the Federal Republic of Montenegro begins. There is a good deal of criticism of the federal system, many senior officials complaining that it multiplies bureaucracy and prevents the emergence of an integral Yugoslav citizen. But at the same time they admit that it is necessary, because it deadens the clan rivalries of the past and eliminates such sores in the body politic as the continual squabbles between, for example, Serbs and Croats which bedevilled Yugoslav politics for decades before the war.

The coast is wilder and more open. There are few islands and the mountains crowd down to the sea. The main towns are Budva, Bar and Ulcinj. There are several flourishing tourist resorts, at Sv. Stefan, Petrovac, Sutomore and some smaller places.

Budva used to be a tiny walled city on a spit of land jutting into the sea with a curious precipitous island-rock just in front of the harbour, too shallow for any save small vessels. Its origins go back to classical times, but it was unruly under the Venetians who limited the number of houses in the city and of persons who might live there. Though sacked a number of times by the Turks, it has preserved its mediaeval aspect and its miniature ninth-century cathedral.

All this is still as it used to be. I spent a night recently in one of the old houses of the walled city, which was cool, spacious and quiet, save for amorous cats, after the night-revellers in the kafana below had gone home. It was a typical example of Montenegrin hospitality. I had rendered a very small service to my hostess, carrying her shopping bag. In return I was given supper and a room to rest in until my ship left at the unearthly hour of 01.15.

Outside the walls things are different. Budva is a very good example of the danger of too rapid tourist development. There are three large and modern tourist hotels and several more are being built, as well as a number of huge resthouses for the employees of large industrial enterprises. There is an air of bustling modernity which does not suit the silent and lovely bays. Development has gone too far, as it has at Lapad near Dubrovnik and one or two other places. But it has still far to go before it can compete with the birdcage hotels and fairground amusements of much of the Italian coast opposite.

Beyond Budva a long, sandy beach curves away towards Miločer and Sv. Stefan, the pride of the Montenegrin tourist industry. Miločer was once the summer palace of the Queen-mother of Yugoslavia, with magnificent gardens and solid stone buildings for the royal suite, which are being converted into an annexe to the hotel. Since it was built as a palace the conversion has led to a certain number of teething troubles, but it is a lovely place to stay.

Just beyond Miločer is the new and luxurious hotel of Sv. Stefan. This used to be a tiny fortress city on an island connected to the mainland by a narrow causeway. It was the capital of the Paštrovići, a union of twelve Montenegrin clans which lived along the coastland from Luštica to Bar. Though more often under foreign rule than independent, they had a long tradition of egalitarian rule and usually managed to ensure that this was respected by their conquerors. Sv. Stefan itself was built and fortified about the end of the fourteenth century with booty seized by the Paštrovići from the Turks who were returning from a raid on Kotor. The Turks repaid this compliment by destroying the city during the Cyprus War of 1570–3, but it was rebuilt with Venetian aid. However, the little island was inhabited long before it became the raiders' citadel. There are still remnants of some Orthodox chapels built in the time of Sv. Sava, but unfortunately only the walls remain and they are of little interest.

Between the wars Sv. Stefan was almost deserted and when, about eight or nine years ago, it was decided to convert the whole island into a hotel, there were only eighteen families left on it. They were given houses on the mainland. One old man is the present guardian of the tiny chapels, and he gave me a very accurate account of the great deeds of his forbears.

There has been much discussion about the reconstruction of Sv. Stefan. But the fact remains that without it the island would now be only a heap of ruins. It has been done carefully and reverently, each little house being an apartment with all modern conveniences. Many of them directly overlook the sea, and an American visitor is said to have caught his breakfast each morning from his bedroom window. It seems a difficult feat, though just possible. *Se non e vero.* . . .

Today Sv. Stefan is the showpiece of the Yugoslav tourist

The city of Sv. Stefan in Montenegro, now transformed into a hotel

industry. Many famous artists and writers spend the summer there, and the prices are commensurate. But after a rather indifferent dinner there I was forced to remember the words of the Montenegrin official: 'It is easy to build a magnificent tourist attraction; the difficulty is to staff it. . . .'

For myself, I do not like big hotels, however luxurious and romantic, so I stayed in the tiny fisherman's house built by my friend the Yugoslav writer Erih Koš in the nearby village of Pržno. It is right on the seashore and a little path, through vineyards and gardens, leads up to the broad ribbon of the Magistrale. Beyond that is the Orthodox monastery of Plašvica and the steep mountain slopes. One of the two churches of the monastery dates from the eleventh century, but the frescoes are much damaged and are only worth a visit by those who have not seen the great frescoed churches of Serbia and Macedonia. So I trudged on up the hillsides in order to visit one – any one – of the mountain villages that look so romantic from the seashore, lone eyries perched high upon the cliffs. The path was narrow, steep and very stony. The sun was blistering. The way seemed endless. After about two hours' scramble I reached the village of Djenaši. It was completely deserted, save for one very old woman who looked like the village sorceress. None the less her house, the only one inhabited, had electric light. The stone houses of the deserted village were large, their walls and roofs intact, their threshing floors overgrown with grasses but otherwise neat and unencumbered. Around them were flowers and fruit-trees and tiny deserted fields. A wonderful place to get a fine house for nothing, at least for those young and strong enough to do their shopping after a two-hour scramble on foot or donkey-back. For there is no road. All the inhabitants had left to find work in Budva, in Belgrade or even in America, Australia, West Germany or England. At the Plašvica monastery a young boy, hearing that I was from England, asked for news of his cousin Vido and showed me an address in Bradford.

When I got back to my house and told the old grandmother next door where I had been she was astonished. No-one went there now. She herself had been born in Djenaši but had not visited it for years. In all that walk of many miles in the mountains

I had spoken to only two persons. When I described them, she said that they were her cousins.

As one approaches Ulcinj the mountains rise in fantastic confusion, range behind range, as if a child were drawing and refused to leave the smallest space unoccupied by some rugged, clear-cut peak. The brilliant sunlight picks out the details of the Ulcinj citadel, close to the water's edge. From a distance it looks rather like a bedraggled Dubrovnik, but with some subtle differences that only become clear as one approaches.

For Ulcinj is no longer Dalmatia. All the other cities of the coast have a certain similarity, due to the influence of Italy and the West. Ulcinj has none. It is of a different world.

Its history has taken quite a different course. It was a city of the Colchians – once again the distant shadow of Medea! – and later an important city of the vague Illyrian Empire of Agron and of Teuta, that stretched from Šibenik to Lesh (Alessio in Albania). It was mentioned by Pliny as Olcinium and was transferred from its earlier site a few miles up the coast to its present one under Justinian in the sixth century, for fear of the Avar invasions. In the eighth century it was taken and held by the Saracens, and the nearby hill of Mavrijan (Moorish) probably preserves a memory of that time. In the first half of the ninth century the Emperor Basil I cleared the seas of these pirates, and for the next three centuries Ulcinj was ruled sometimes by Greek, sometimes by Slav, rulers. At the great period of the Nemanja dynasty in Serbia it appears to have been held by a relative of theirs, Vukan; and his son, George, in 1242 is referred to as Rex Georgius dominus Ulcinii. In the same year it was unsuccessfully attacked by the Tatars. Fresh complaints of piracy broke out in 1281, but during the fourteenth and fifteenth centuries it was still in Christian hands, sometimes Venetian, sometimes Slav.

But all this is the dry bones of history and has left no mark on Ulcinj save some ruined walls in the deserted citadel and an inscription of the Balša family so corrupt that to my mind it is the fake of some pious patriot.

What gave Ulcinj its peculiar colour and the most splendid period of its history was the Turkish conquest of 1571, when it was taken by Uluch Ali, Bey of Algiers, an ally of the Sultan

Selim II in his war against Venice. After Lepanto, Uluch Ali became Turkish admiral with the title of Kilidji (the sword) and his corsairs settled in Ulcinj. From that time onwards Ulcinj has been, and remains, a Moslem sea-port.

All through the seventeenth century these corsairs harried the ports and shipping of southern Dalmatia. In January 1624 they entered the Boka and destroyed Perast, and attempted to do so again in 1687, but were defeated by the Perastines and Montene-grins, who killed almost half of them and forced them to disgorge their booty. Then the famous corsair, Hajdar Karamidjia, of Greek descent, became captain of the city and successfully defended it against the Venetians in 1696. It was he who built the pasha's mosque and the fountain near it, which still exist.

These corsairs wars were rendered more ferocious by the fact that captured Moslems had to ransom themselves with Christian slaves and kept, so to speak, a stock on hand. They did not want to share the fate of Dinko Kampsa who could not do this and was stoned to death on the island opposite Budva.

The corsairs of Ulcinj rapidly adopted the Albanian customs and language, and it is probable that the so-called Albanian sailors used by Venice in her wars with the Uskoks were from Ulcinj, as the real Albanian is a poor sailor.

Many famous pirate names are still preserved in the annals of Ulcinj; for example, Hadji Alija, whose base of operations was near Valona and whose spirit, sword in hand, is still said to haunt the waves. Also Liko Cen, who was commissioned by the Sultan to free the Adriatic of the still more notorious Greek pirate Hara-lampija of Messalonghi. This he succeeded in doing, and entered the Golden Horn in triumph with Haralampija's body tied to his bowsprit. For this, his own sins were pardoned and he ended his life as a merchant. In the eighteenth century a chronicler writes: 'In Ulcinj live some six thousand persons, pirates, who call themselves merchants and live, after the manner of Algiers, on plunder.' Towards the end of the sixteenth century Serb names also appear among them. When the notorious Mehmed Bušatlija became pasha of Skadar, however, Ulcinj became a little republic. He attacked the city to defend trade, scuttled its ships and forced it to submit. The corsair days of Ulcinj were over.

But though Ulcinj was a factor of importance in the southern Adriatic, it was to the sultans merely a distant and unruly seaport on the confines of Islam.

All Moslem towns have a certain sameness. But, after some time in Dalmatia, the Moslem atmosphere of Ulcinj comes with all the force of novelty. To find a sea-coast town with eight mosques in working order and heaven knows how many others in ruins is surprising. But for my part I prefer to walk in the former citadel. It occupies the whole peninsula that forms one of the horns of the harbour.

In all the vast extent of the fortress only two or three families still live, in tumbledown palaces. It is a strange feeling to go there in the evening, for while the fortress as a whole is empty and desolate, the abode only of ghosts, the glassless windows of these few inhabited houses are lit with electric light.

There are few inscriptions or coats-of-arms, for the great period of Ulcinj was under the corsairs, who took little stock of heraldry. Now and again you will find a Christian monogram or a shield from Venetian times, but rarely. The Balša inscription, as I have said before, looks like a fake. Indeed, the only indubitable trace of pre-Venetian rule that I could find was a fine piece of Slavo-Byzantine ornamentation built into the steps of the main church, afterwards mosque, of the fortress. It, too, is now ruined and deserted.

The final destruction of the citadel dates from the Montenegrin war of 1878.

It is a fascinating, but somewhat perilous, walk at night, for the battered walls may suddenly open onto a sheer drop to the water beneath. It is not hard to recreate there the shapes of Liko Cen, of Uluch Ali Kilidji or the uneasy ghost of Hadji Alija. Probably it is too late to repair the fortress now, but none the less it adds an air of vanished splendour to the little town, contrasting oddly with the other horn of the harbour, where there are modern hotels, the new challenging the old across the still waters of the bay.

CHAPTER X

Back Door to Montenegro

The whirlpool market – The lake of Skadar – Background to Montenegro – Petar Petrović-Njegoš: prince-bishop and poet – Wartime episode at Podgorica – Andrijevica and the Rugovo gorge – The Albanian retreat – Peć and the Albanians – The Peć Patriarchate.

Bus travel in Yugoslavia usually starts at an unearthly hour in the morning, since the long-distance buses carry the mail. But it is not quite so bad as it sounds. For one thing, the summer dawns are marvellous and it is well worth a little discomfort to be up in time to see them. Also they are pleasantly cool and the land breathes a freshness that one does not find later in the day.

Journeys by bus are casual and good-humoured and seldom without their amusing side. I recall an instance in the Sanjak when the fan-belt broke and, after some argument, was mended with a belt borrowed from a travelling imam, who spent the rest of the journey holding up his precarious trousers. For the Yugoslavs are masters in the art of improvisation, and the fact that a bus looks as if it were tied up with string, and very probably is, is no indication that it will not go.

Of course with the nationalization of transport a good deal of this happy-go-lucky travelling has disappeared. The grim spectre of bureaucracy looms darkly in the background. But these general remarks are still true enough on the provincial lines. Of course they do not apply to the main tourist routes whose buses start on time, arrive more or less on time and have a fixed tariff. They offer greater speed and comfort, but less amusement. The less-frequented bus routes have, however, a definite character of their own. The journeys are long and a companionship of the road is quickly established.

This Montenegrin outpost land is one of the wildest in Yugo-slavia. The road follows a long, winding valley with, now and again, tantalizing glimpses of silent and lovely bays. The first stop is at Stari (Old) Bar.

This, too, is a deserted city. At a distance it looks magnificent: a walled city with a large Venetian fortress, built on the edge of a little ravine and guarding the pass through the mountains. It was evidently a place of some importance, being of considerable size, but now looks like the scene of a Gothic novel, for ivy (a rare thing in these parts) and other climbing plants have covered the buildings, so that it has not the rugged desolation of the fortress of Ulcinj. It, too, was destroyed in the Montenegrin wars, though it was probably in decadence before that time. The present village – for one can no longer call it a city – is built outside the walls, with the main street, which is most surprisingly stone-paved throughout, ending abruptly at the wall of the fortress.

The new village of Stari Bar is a strange transition from the purely oriental to the modern Montenegrin. The main street is clean and well arranged, but the side streets are squalid and casual. Incidentally, one first comes across here what are usually known as Constantinople eggs. These are no more than ordinary hard-boiled eggs, but boiled very slowly in strong coffee-grounds. The flavour penetrates the shell, and so does the colour, so that they turn, inside and out, to an unexpected and somewhat disconcerting coffee colour.

Modern Bar is quite different. It is planned, brisk, enterprising and up-to-date, a minor triumph of modern communications. The magnificent bay is now a busy harbour and the centuries-old olive groves produce the best oil in Yugoslavia. But few people stop here; it is essentially a transit port. For one thing it is on the Magistrale, which has become the backbone of the whole Yugoslav coast, and for another it is the terminal point of the new broad-gauge Adriatic railway which links it with the federal capital of Titograd and will eventually link it with Belgrade. It is a fantastically ambitious enterprise considering the mountainous nature of the country and one which has been talked about for generations. It replaces the tiny narrow-gauge railway to Virpazar whose serpentines and convolutions were so lengthy that a young man could cover the distance more rapidly on foot, a feat frequently done for a bet. He could not do it now.

Bar also has direct sea-links with Bari on the Italian coast opposite and in 1965 a car-ferry was started which brings tourists and
their cars to the Magistrale within a few hours.

Now, there are two land routes to Virpazar. The best is by the
Magistrale and the new branch from Petrovac to Titograd. The
road is good and the journey can be made in a comparatively
short time. The older route scales the Sutorman mountains,
stopping at tiny mountain villages. It is rougher but even more
scenic. From the summit there is a last marvellous view of the
perfect semi-circle of Bar harbour before the downward plunge
in ever-closer spirals towards Virpazar and the Lake of Skadar.

The first view of Virpazar, the 'Whirlpool Market', and the
Lake of Skadar is an experience. It looks not so much a lake as a
sunken world. The karst hills run straight down into the water,
which is still and shallow, with the green of water-weeds showing
through and trees growing in it in desultory lines. In the stiller
reaches the surface is covered with a dark green alga. Only in the
distance is the lake clear and blue.

Virpazar itself is almost surrounded by water, with the roads
forming causeways binding it to the higher land around. For the
Lake of Skadar is really a flooded polje, with the higher hillocks
standing out of it as islands. A drop of 2 or 3 metres in the water-
level would make it possible to reclaim almost a third of the area
and to rescue for cultivation many broad acres that have been
rendered valueless since the silting up of the river Bojana forced
the lake to its present level. Then the real lake, that section which
looks blue and not green, would become a friend and not an enemy
of man, and this part of Montenegro, which at present has to
import grain, would become a great producing centre. It is a
grandiose plan, and not really as difficult or as expensive as it at
first appears.

The new road and railway cross the lake on a long causeway,
starting from Virpazar and cutting across the northern end of the
island of Vranjina. It has brought comparative prosperity to the
formerly rather dirty and uninteresting little town. Today it is a
pleasant little oasis in the harsh stone and scrub of the mountain-
sides. It has a pleasant tree-lined square, a little landing-stage
whence the lake steamers ply to distant villages or take tourists

for joy-rides and, on Fridays, a colourful little market on the lakeside where huge carp gape hopefully at prospective buyers. Many
are split, salted and sun-dried for winter fare. Moreover, the little
hotel, which I cursed so wholeheartedly before the war has
become a simple but welcoming hostel where one may eat one's
carp and sip one's coffee at the edge of the water.

Virpazar has one of the many castles that used to ring the lake,
ever in dispute between Montenegrins, Turks and the pasha of
Skadar in Albania. At the foot of its ruined walls there is a fine,
rather modernistic, memorial to the first partisans who fell there in
1941. For Virpazar justifies its name. It has been a frequent storm
centre. It was here that the terrible Montenegrin Vespers started;
and it was here, in 1941, that the resistance began in Montenegro
with the ambushing of an Italian convoy. I was a prisoner at
Podgorica (now Titograd) at the time, and the consequences were
violent and immediate.

The new road and rail causeway runs straight across the lake,
close to the fortress-island of Lesendro, the key to its domination,
and the northern end of the island of Vranjina, a bare and drome-
dary islet supposed to have been at one time the capital of Zeta,
the predecessor of Montenegro, but which now supports only one
picturesque fishing village and a multitude of snakes. The fishermen have to manoeuvre their tiny boats through a narrow under-
pass in the causeway.

South of Vranjina, far out in the lake and, on clear days, within
sight of the Albanian city of Skadar, is Snake Island, now a heap
of ruins, which was at one time a political prison and a place of
exile. It can only be seen by boat.

This is in the deep central part of the lake. But north of Vranjina
the lake is shallow, with intricate channels amid the reeds, the
home of countless varieties of water-birds. I have seen herons,
bitterns and cormorants and once, wonder of wonders, a flight
(what is the proper noun of assembly for these birds?) of pelicans.
There were about twenty of them, flying low in close formation.
It was a remarkable sight, for the pelican is a shy and rare bird,
preferring the most isolated parts of the lake, and does not visit
it every year. I had often heard tell of them, but repeated dis-
appointments had almost made me doubt their existence.

At the northern end of the lake is Rijeka Crnojevića, a picturesque little place on the Crnojević river which is a branch of the Lake of Skadar, winding between tall cliffs of bare or scrub-covered karst of that peculiar Montenegrin blackness. It has a strange and extraordinary beauty; the still waters, the navigation marks topped by the nests of martins, and the frowning black mountains and twisting channel seem like a stage set for the coming of Siegfried's ship to Iceland. The surface of the water is dead and unrippled, covered with water-plants, leaving only a narrow strip for the passage of the lake steamers. At certain seasons it is a blaze of white waterlilies, as gay and decorative as a Japanese print, so that the amateur art-critic has his work cut out to identify the celestial artist. An artist could paint a wonderful picture of the Crnojević river. But he had better exhibit it as a

The Rijeka Crnojevića leading into the lake of Skadar

work of fancy. No-one who has not seen it would believe it to be true.

Rijeka Crnojevića is built on the first spot where the mountains relent. Here man has, perhaps unconsciously, added to the beauty of the landscape by building two stone bridges across the river, perfect in proportion and mellowed by age to harmonize with the dark cliffs. They were built for utility but have had beauty thrust upon them. Nearby is the monastery of Obod, founded by Ivan Crnojević, the great hero of the Montenegrins, where the first printing-press of the Slav lands was erected in 1485. There are still extant a few pages of its work, but it had a short life, its metal being required for sterner work, the casting of bullets.

From Rijeka Crnojevića the road runs west and east, to Cetinje and to Titograd.

For many visitors Cetinje means Montenegro. They come up on the Boka or Budva coaches, look for a few moments at the tiny former capital and then go away again. For, since the war, Cetinje has ceased to be the capital of Montenegro. That honour has passed to new, enterprising and progressive Titograd. Consequently there is a bitter feud between the citizens of the old and new capitals, the more bitter insofar as they are the centres of different clans. Perhaps from a visitor's standpoint, however, that is all that Cetinje is worth. It is not in itself a very interesting town. Its charm lies in the wild grandeur of its surroundings and in its associations. It is only interesting because it was once a capital, so that there are palaces, government offices and legations on a doll's-house scale. The palace is interesting to those who can recreate the characters of vanished worthies from inanimate things, but there are many places besides Cetinje that have been important in the history of Montenegro. Today, Cetinje is sleepy and undistinguished, a city of pensioners.

The history of Montenegro has been one of continual struggle. Its earlier days were a welter of various petty princes, confusing and without great interest; yet it can claim with a certain amount of justice to have been the earliest independent Serbian state. For, needless to say, the Montenegrins are Serbs, and claim to be the purest blood of that race. But it is only in the fifteenth century that it begins to be of interest to a wider world. After the fall of the

Serbian Empire in the fourteenth century and of the Serbian despotate and independent Bosnia a few years later, it was the last stronghold of liberty of the South Slav peoples. So it remained for about three hundred years until the first Serbian insurrection of 1804. There were preserved the traditions of the Serbian race in their purest form, and from time to time families of these gallant highlanders re-peopled the devastated Šumadija (Central Serbia). At that time it was ruled by the Crnojević family, whose most famous member was known as Ivan Beg. It was he who first left the mountain fastnesses of Ostrog and Žabljak and descended into the plain of Cetinje to found that city which, until the liberation of 1918, remained the capital of independent Montenegro. He also inflicted the first of a long series of defeats on the Ottoman armies, which tried to subdue the Black Mountain. (I have used the familiar Montenegro throughout; the Serbo-Croat name is Crna Gora – both mean Black Mountain.)

From time to time the Montenegrins acknowledged a shadowy overlordship of the Turks and in earlier times of the Venetians, but neither had at any time any effective rule. True, the Turks destroyed Cetinje, but then had once more to retreat. The truth was that, before the building of modern roads, the Black Mountain was impregnable. A small army the Montenegrins could defeat; a large one could not live in that stony and barren land. Montenegro became synonymous with South Slav freedom.

After the extinction of the Crnojević family, Montenegro was ruled by its bishops and by a rather ill-defined authority called the gubernador. But with the rise of the greatest of the Montenegrin families, Petrović-Njegoš, these two authorities were combined, so that Montenegro was ruled by a sort of theocratic autocracy, the line of descent being from uncle to nephew. Only later did it become a kingdom with a normal line of succession. Gradually it increased its tiny territory. Always it had a burning interest in Yugoslav liberation, always a hatred of the Turks. Unruly and undisciplined, but brave and enthusiastic, it rendered great services to the Yugoslav ideal. But dynastic quarrels embittered the issue in the late nineteenth century, and during the First World War King Nikola flirted with the Central Powers. Finally the people of Montenegro deposed the dynasty and declared their adherence to the Kingdom of the Serbs, Croats and Slovenes at Podgorica in 1918, and the gallant history of Montenegro became merged in that of Yugoslavia. The Karageorgević dynasty was closely allied to the former Montenegrin royal house. King Alexander was born in Cetinje.

The greatest ruler of Montenegro was the Prince-Bishop Petar Petrović-Njegoš. He was also the greatest poet of the Yugoslav language, surpassing even Gundulić in the power and sweep of his characterization and the beauty of his language. He writes in a very terse style, a little reminiscent of Browning and equally difficult to read. His best known works are poetic dramas, describing the two most vivid events in Montenegrin history. The finest of them, 'The Mountain Wreath' (Gorski Vijenac), describes the Montenegrin Vespers. Islam had begun to penetrate even among the Montenegrins, whose whole existence had been bound up with the struggle for the Cross. Heroic measures were decided upon, and at a given moment all Moslems in the country were given their choice of conversion or the sword. The outbreak began at Virpazar. But the poem is remarkable not so much for its narration as for the character-drawing of the leaders, both Moslem and Christian, the clash of ideals and the real depth and feeling of the verse. Many Yugoslavs even today quote some rhyming proverb, without knowing that they are quoting from 'The Mountain Wreath'.

The second drama describes the short rule of Stefan the Small, a political adventurer who came to Montenegro and ruled there for a time, by giving out that he was the murdered Tsar Peter III who had escaped his enemies. The Montenegrins accepted him, having always had a fondness for the Russians, whom they considered as the greatest of the Slav peoples and their especial protectors. The wisdom and good sense of his rule were sufficient to prove that his claims were untrue!

A third poem, 'The Light of the Microcosm', is Miltonic and visionary, but now little read.

This long period of continual struggle against the Turk has had a great influence on the character of the Montenegrin. He has so long been a warrior that he now finds it difficult to be anything else, and still regards the trader and the artisan as beings of a somewhat lower order. He has, in fact, preserved in a primitive form the spirit of the mediaeval knight, with all its virtues and very many of its prejudices. He makes a first-class soldier and administrator, but a poor subordinate. Therefore the Montenegrin outside his own country either rises rapidly to a position of trust and influence or becomes the most morally corrupt of all the Yugoslavs. It is a question of character and of education. Those who have the character to apply their code of honour and heroism to the complexities of the modern world become great men; those who forsake it rapidly acquire a Western polish and Western vices, but little else.

The heroic code of the Montenegrins is deeply respected by the other Yugoslavs, but it is also the occasion of a good deal of dry humour. Jokes against the Montenegrins in Yugoslavia are almost as common as against the Scots in England.

A peasant story tells how, when God was distributing the stones on the Days of Creation, the Devil slit open the bag as he was passing over Montenegro. It certainly describes the landscape. But, none the less, a trip through Montenegro is extremely beautiful. The mountains are high and impressive, the poljes little green patches of fertility. The rivers, rich in trout, rush foaming through picturesque gorges. Almost at every season there is something to lend a touch of colour to the grim landscape. At one time it is the rich flame of the pomegranates; at another the brilliant yellow of the pumpkins.

This is the Montenegro that most tourists know. But the eastern districts are different. There is less stone and more forest. It is at the mountain-saddle between Cetinje and Titograd that the Mediterranean flora ceases and the continental begins. There are no more figs and olives and pomegranates, but forests of pine and an occasional poplar which give a hint of the typical landscape of Macedonia.

Podgorica I probably knew better than any city in Yugoslavia. I was held there for several months during the war as a prisoner of the Italian army. But their supervision was somewhat lax, and once in the maze of tiny streets that used to be known – I know not why – as Catalonia, it was a bold carabiniere who would have dared to look for me. It was a strange and eventful time, and before it ended I had spent two years in camps and prisons in Albania, Italy and Germany.

But Podgorica no longer exists. The old town, the largest in Montenegro, was pretty battered when I was its prisoner. Subsequent bombardments reduced it to ruins. It is now called Titograd (the city of Tito) and is a completely new city with, incidentally, a first-class hotel. Nothing remains of the city I knew except the gorge of the Morača river and a few stones of the old citadel where Stefan Nemanja was born. Older inhabitants remembered the Jadran kafana where I had been held prisoner and even its one-legged proprietor, Stefan Radonić. It is characteristic of the Montenegrins that they all insisted on knowing the name of the man who had betrayed my presence there to the Italian authorities, so that tardy vengeance might be sought. But I knew that he had been shot many years before for some other act of treachery and a possibly awkward incident was avoided.

From Titograd there is a bus service through Montenegro to Peć and the Kosmet – the autonomous region of Kosovo and Metohija. It is a marvellous though tiring journey. I have made the trip several times, usually in mid-summer, but even so the bus twice climbs to the snowline, at Trešnjevik and at Čakor. The first stop is Andrijevica.

There could hardly be a greater contrast than between Titograd and Andrijevica. Andrijevica is built of wood among forests; Titograd of stone among stones. In fact, Andrijevica already foreshadows the little wood-built towns of the Sanjak and Bosnia. It is not, in itself, a very interesting place, but it is worth mentioning that it is a good centre for some of the best hunting and fishing in all Yugoslavia.

The road then passes over the Čakor Pass, about 6,500 feet above sea-level, and descends into the Rugovo gorge. The high mountain uplands around the pass are fascinating, the meadows gay with cyclamen, huge buttercups and 6-foot high foxgloves. If you make the trip in summer, you may catch sight of a bačilo, one of the reed-built summer villages where the shepherds live in the fair season, feeding their flocks on the rich grass.

The descent into the Rugovo Gorge is awe-inspiring. The

mountain torrent of the Bistrica rages below and the road serpentines downwards within the gorge itself. One is well advised to make the journey by open car, for the buses are covered and in the depths of the gorge one cannot see the mountain peaks without leaning dangerously out of the window.

My last trip across the Čakor was made in the opposite direction, from Peć to Titograd. The bus was old and crowded and started at the appalling hour of five a.m. Behind me was a group of six gipsies, noisy, raggle-taggle and rather smelly. It did not seem a good beginning. But after we had been about an hour on the journey, they began to sing. They sang beautifully, using the old Serb and Macedonian folk-tunes but making up the words as they sang to suit the occasion. Some of them were pretty bawdy and soon almost everyone in the bus had become the target for their wit. It is rare today to hear the old tunes sung so well, and the seven hours of the trip passed rapidly. It was a remarkable and rewarding experience.

This road was only built in 1925. So it is rather horrifying to recall that it was through this gorge that the Second Serbian Army had to retreat in the depths of the hard winter of 1915. The whole army was reorganized into groups for mountain warfare, and the heavy guns and equipment were destroyed or buried near Peć to prevent them falling into the hands of the enemy. The army was followed by large numbers of the civilian population, including children. It was the first stage of that terrible 'Albanian retreat' which cost so many lives, but which saved the Serbian Army to fight again and finally lead the breakthrough on the Salonica front two years later. There are many harrowing stories of the retreat, when the soldiers, harassed by the Albanians, sold the shirts off their backs for a morsel of dry maize-bread, for paper money had no longer any value. The story of the march through Albania and the final regrouping on the island of Corfu is one of the most terrible in a history that has no lack of tragedies.

It was at this time that the lovely and melancholy tune 'Tamo daleko' became so well known. It was not originally a folk-song, but has become one.

> *There over yonder*
> *Far beyond the sea*

There lies my homeland,
There lies Serbia . . .

Almost in the mouth of the gorge lies the Peć Patriarchate and, just beyond, the town of Peć.

Here at Peć one already finds that oriental flavour that persists right through Old Serbia and Macedonia. The streets in the older part of the city are all more or less the same, as all the houses open on to an inner court and show nothing to the outer world save an eyeless wall, with perhaps one tiny latticed window for the very mild Moslem flirtations, where the lover can scarcely get a glimpse of his beloved. I have among my friends a Moslem Beg from Peć, so have had a chance of seeing one of these houses from within. It was lovely sitting there on the čardak-balcony, especially in the velvety darkness of the night. The garden was pleasant with the sound of running water, and somewhere in the poplars a nightingale was singing. We sat there, chatting and drinking rose-cordial, until dawn.

At Peć one comes into contact with the Albanians. For it is one of the principal towns of the Autonomous District of Kosmet (Kosovo-Metohija), created after the war to help to solve the Albanian minority problem in this area. Possibly Albanians lived here in very early times – the professors still argue on the point – but those living there now are descendants of comparative newcomers from the late seventeenth century onwards. Now they constitute a good half of the population of the area. They have their own press, schools and cultural institutions, and much has been done in the Kosmet to systematize their recently revised but very ancient language. The curious clipped tones of the Shqiptar speech are to be heard almost as frequently as Serbo-Croat and official notices are in both languages.

I know the Albanians well. After the episode at Podgorica I was in prison at Tirana for some time, where I received the most friendly and hospitable treatment from the leading Albanians, many of whom were in the same prison with me. As a people, they are a remarkably sympathetic lot. They are not industrious, but that is the fault of their history. They are, however, manly, good-humoured, with a ready wit, and strictly honest. They have a code of honour which, though their present Government is doing its best to destroy it, has served them for a thousand years or so. They are sober and satisfied with little. They are hospitable and welcome any stranger whom they respect; to others they are reserved and contemptuous. As individuals they have the finest of the virtues and the more manly of the vices. Their women are moral, reserved and almost always strictly virtuous. In the house they have a position of esteem; outside it they are still in subjection, which may also be laid at the door of history. Often, when one has a chance of seeing them at all, as in the mountain villages, they are, when young, extremely beautiful.

But one comes to Peć to see the Patriarchate.

The seat of the Serbian Orthodox Church was moved here in 1346, when seven-gated Žiča was too close to the Hungarian frontier, in the reign of Tsar Dušan. It was in that year also that the Serbian Archbishop was advanced to the rank of a Patriarch and crowned Dušan as Emperor of Serbs, Greeks and Albanians,

Sv. Nikola; from a fresco in the Patriarchate at Peć

the future ruler of the Byzantine Empire had not the Turks come
and destroyed his wide-flung plans. He was crowned at Skopje,
not only by the Serbian Patriarch, but also by the Bulgarian
Patriarch and the Greek Archbishop of Ohrid.

But the role of Peć was to be less brilliant, though equally
glorious. Under Turkish rule, the Christian peasants became
raja – that is to say, subject peoples more or less in the position
of serfs. The temporal power was little by little destroyed. The
only national institution left was the Church, which was a centre
of national feeling made doubly strong by the sharp religious
cleavage between Moslem and Christian. But it was too dangerous
a centre. Shortly after the fall of Smederevo, in 1459, the Serbian
Patriarchate was abolished by the Turks, and the spiritual power
exercised by the Greek Archbishops of Ohrid. The national
feeling was still kept alive by the Serbian priests and even more by
the national epics. The darker side of feudal times was forgotten
and a tradition created of the good old days of freedom.

In 1557, however, the Serbian Patriarchate was again revived
by the Grand Vizier, Mehmed Sokolović, one of the many Serb
Bosnians who had accepted Islam and risen to high rank. He
appointed his relative Makarije, a monk of Hilendar, to be
Patriarch. Thus Peć became once more a national and cultural
centre for the Serbs. The Patriarch was acknowledged as spiritual
chief of his people, and to some extent represented them also in
temporal matters. Churches and monasteries were repaired and
rebuilt and church books copied and distributed. It was a time of
spiritual regeneration, though on a modest scale as the Church
was never allowed to grow too powerful under Turkish rule.

After Makarije's death in 1547 his successors began to dream
dreams of national liberation. They entered into negotiations
with the Western Powers, Austria and Russia, and stirred up
revolts against Turkish rule, such as that of the Voevoda Grdan
in the Hercegovina. Missions were sent to the Courts of Russia
and the Moldavian Prince Bessarab, and even to Rome.

Almost all the Peć Patriarchs became involved in these patriotic
intrigues, and matters came to a head during the Austro-Turkish
wars of the seventeenth century, when Serb volunteers actively
assisted the Austrian troops. The Patriarch Arsenius III was

forced to flee, and in 1690 crossed the Danube into Austrian
territory with a large number of Serb families. This was known
as the Great Migration and was a turning-point in the history of
the Serbian Orthodox Church. The successor of Arsenius, Kalinik
I, succeeded in calming the outraged Turks, but his successor
attempted yet another rebellion during the Austro-Turkish war
of 1737 and only managed to save his life by flight. The power of
the Peć Patriarchs declined rapidly, and in 1766 the Patriarchate
was finally abolished. From then until the Serbian insurrection
of 1804 most of the higher clergy in the Serbian lands under
Ottoman rule were Greeks.

Incidentally it was after the Great Migration that large numbers
of Albanians descended from their mountains to the districts
around Peć and occupied the deserted lands of the fugitives.

The Patriarchate, however, continued to exist at Sremski
Karlovci in the Dual Kingdom and still carried out its role as a
centre for the Serbs, this time for those under Austro-Hungarian
rule. Peć only returned to something of its former glory after the
First World War liberation. It was in Peć that the first Orthodox
Patriarch of united Yugoslavia was enthroned in 1924.

The building itself lies in the mouth of the Rugovo gorge so
that the mountains make a frame around its squat cupolas. It is a
strange building, composed not of one but several churches. It is
full of frescoes, of halls leading nowhere in particular, and
changing floor levels. In the course of a stormy history it has been
restored, rebuilt and destroyed again by local pashas several times.
In the seventeenth and eighteenth centuries it was even encircled
by high walls and turned into a fortress. Also its frescoes were
repainted many times, so that little remains of the magnificence
of the original twelfth- and thirteenth-century work. But of that
little, some parts are of extraordinary interest, more especially
the soot-blackened Family Tree of the Nemanjas, from the Great
Župan Stefan Nemanja himself down to Stefan Dečanski and his
three sons Dušan, Dušman and Simeon. The whole building is
steeped in history.

CHAPTER XI

Holy Ground: Men, Monarchs and Marko in Serbia and Macedonia

The battle of Kosovo – The Yugoslav heroic ballads – Guslari – Marko, hero of the Serbs – Sv. Sava, greatest of the Nemanjas – The ritual of the slava – Restoring the monasteries – Lake Ohrid, cradle of Slav Christianity – Mediaeval fresco painters – The Nemanja dynasty – An original architectural style – Studenica, Sopoćani, Dečani – Markovgrad, a ghost city of the Balkans – The long way to Matejić – The churches of the despots – The Serbian insurrection – Oplenac.

This is holy ground. Only a few miles from Peć is the Field of Blackbirds – Kosovo Polje – where the Turkish forces inflicted a crushing defeat on the Serbo-Bosnian confederation on Vidovdan, 1389. It was the downfall of the Serbian power, which did not recover from the blow for more than five hundred years. It is true that for some years after Kosovo a Serbian state continued to exist, and its final overthrow was the fall of Smederevo in 1459, but the Serbian peasant has perhaps a clearer view of history than the historians when he tells you: 'If God meant well to me, Lazar would not have been killed on Kosovo.'

There is much argument about the actual events of the battle. The great king of Bosnia, Tvrtko, seems to have considered it a victory, and sent letters announcing the downfall of the Turks to the cities of Dalmatia and even Italy. But then he was not present. The role of 'the traitor', Vuk Branković, son-in-law of Lazar, appears to be entirely unhistorical. But the events of that day have become so over-crusted by legend and tradition that it is hard to tell even from more or less contemporary historians which is which. Some Russian monks passing through Serbia and near Kosovo on their way to Constantinople at the time of the battle do not mention it at all.

However, none of this really matters. Let the professors try to solve these problems, over which the dust of history has laid so thick a covering. The actors are dead and their deeds or misdeeds of little import. What matters is the Kosovo legend that lives undimmed in the minds of the people to the present day.

It has been preserved in the most beautiful cycle of the heroic ballads. In the long night of Turkish oppression few men could read and write, but many could remember and sing. The legends of old times and the stirring combats of more recent history were preserved in the form of long epic poems, handed down by word of mouth from father to son and recited by wandering guslari, players of the gusle, a one-stringed fiddle with a melancholy and monotonous wail which acts as a sort of bourdon to the chant of the minstrel. Often blind, they would go from village to village, reciting the deeds of kings and heroes and keeping alive the pride of ancestry and the hope of deliverance.

No one knows exactly how old these songs may be. There are references to them in early Byzantine writers, and the more cultivated poets of Dalmatia often quoted from them in the days of the Renaissance. But not much remains of these very early epics, and that for the most part of little real beauty or value. The great flowering of the Serbian epic stems from the years about, or just after, Kosovo, with a second great upsurging of creative force in the years of the first Serbian insurrections, the days of Karageorge, in the early nineteenth century.

There are several types. But one is so predominent that it may well serve for all the others; this is a ten- or eleven-syllable verse into which the Serbian language naturally falls. This was a great aid to memory and improvisation, and some of the guslari knew 50,000 or 60,000 lines. Nor has the tradition or the capacity entirely died out even today when universal compulsory education has sapped the vigour of peasant poetry. I have heard guslari recite in the more out-of-the-way villages, and on one occasion, at Kladovo in East Serbia, one of them improvised to the gusle a long poem about myself.

I have even heard peasant poets singing of the partisan wars, but the spread of education has dulled the oral imagination of these village poets and the new epics have not the vitality and force of the old ones. It is a pity, for the incidents of the partisan wars have much in common with those of the Karageorge rebellion against the Turks. The battle of Sutjeska, for example, would make a magnificent epic. None the less, there is still something of the peasant tradition in the work of those poets who have sung of the partisan struggle. A good deal of this is pedestrian and un-inspired, but there are some noble exceptions. I would cite the best work of Vladimir Nazor and some really moving verses by the young Ivan Goran Kovačić, who was killed by the right-wing četniks in 1943. His poem 'Jama' (The Pit) is a masterpiece.

Luckily for us, the Serbian epics were written down and published at the time of their highest development, just after the Karageorge insurrection, by Vuk Stefan Karadžić, the founder of the modern Serbo-Croat literary language, which was, indeed, based on these epics and on the vigorous speech of the common people. Many other collections have been made since, though Vuk's is not only the first, but also the best. He travelled through the country, taking down the ballads from the mouths of the guslari, especially one most famous amongst them, Filip Višnjić.

These epics should be read, not only for their beauty, which is great, but also for an understanding of Serbia. There are several excellent modern translations of many of them; it would be invidious to make comparisons. But avoid the mawkish senti-mentalities of Bowring or Meredith, men who did not even know the language, but relied, at second hand, on French or German versions. These poems have a hard, sinewy, virile beauty with plenty of sentiment but no sentimentality.

In the cycle of Kosovo we forsake history for legend. A great battle is to be fought. Before it, St Elias appears to Tsar Lazar and gives him the choice of an earthly or a heavenly crown. Tsar Lazar chooses the heavenly kingdom, and the Serbian host goes out to meet the Turks, prepared to die. Before the battle there is a last supper with Lazar and his nobles. The tsar toasts his nobles one by one, till he comes to Miloš Obilić, whom he taunts as:

> *First loyal to me – and at last most false,*
> *Tomorrow thou wilt in battle betray me . . .*

Miloš resents the taunt and swears that he will himself kill the

Turkish sultan. The armies meet and the Serbs are defeated. Miloš, brought captive before the sultan, breaks loose, kills him, and is himself killed. The traitor, on the other hand, is not Miloš Obilić, but the tsar's son-in-law, Vuk Branković, who deserts him on the field.

The battle itself is summarily described. But some of the most lovely of the poems describe the preparation of the heroes for the battle and the reluctance of Tsar Lazar's wife, Princess Milica, to let her husband, father and nine brothers – the nine Jugovići – go to certain death. The two best known of all describe the death from sorrow of the mother of Jugovići and the journey to the battlefield of the Maiden of Kosovo to search among the fallen for her betrothed, Milan of Toplica. The poem ends with a lovely lament:

> . . . *Now betake thee to thy white-walled dwelling,*
> *Do not smear thy skirt and sleeves with bloodstains.*
>
> *When the maiden heard the words he uttered,*
> *Down her cheeks the heavy tear-drops trickled,*
> *Back she wandered to her white-walled dwelling,*
> *Loud laments the beauteous maiden uttered:*
> *'Woe upon me, miserable maiden!*
> *If I laid my hand upon a pine-tree,*
> *Young and green, it would dry up and shrivel.'*
>
> (Trans. Prof. W. A. Morison)

The defeat of 1389 was not the only battle on the Field of Kosovo. A glance at the map will show that in Serbia or Macedonia any full-scale battle between major armies must be fought out on the plain either of Kosovo or Kumanovo. But its memory has endured the longest. Tradition, though it may distort the story of the past, has power to create the story of the future. When the Serb soldiers freed the Field of Kosovo from the Turks in 1912, they knelt and kissed the earth that to them was holy, and whose carpet of blood-red peonies sprang from the blood of the heroes who had died there five hundred years before.

There are still peonies on the Field of Kosovo today; also a Turkish mausoleum claimed, I know not with what right, to be the Tomb of Murad. It has been erected quite close to the marble church of Gračanica, built some sixty odd years before the battle and mentioned often in the cycle of Kosovo. But of Gračanica and the other magnificent churches and monasteries of Serbia and Macedonia we shall speak later in this chapter.

The Kosovo cycle is the best known of the Serbian heroic ballads. But there are others older and some almost as beautiful.

The older ones are unconnected with any cycle, and their origins may well go back into the far-distant past. Sometimes there are echoes of other epic poetry, perhaps stemming from a common source, for example 'Predrag and Nenad' or 'Simeon the Foundling', which recall the legends of the ancient Greeks; 'The Marriage of Maksim Crnojević', with memories of the Nibelungenlied, or 'The Marriage of Tsar Dušan'. These last two, though connected in the poet's mind with historical characters, are purely legendary, the stuff of faery. The best known is 'The Building of Skadar', based on that very ancient belief that a human sacrifice is needed to complete some great work of construction, a superstition that still exists in very attenuated form in the placing of things of value under a foundation stone. Yet even

The monastery-church of Gračanica (1321) on the Field of Kosovo

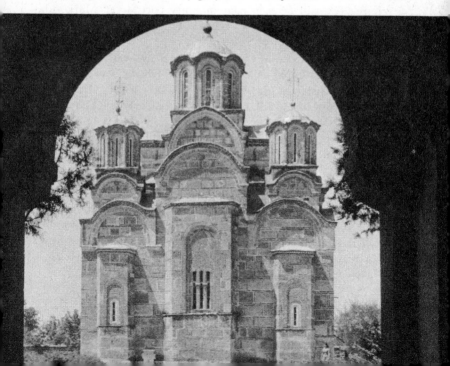

this is connected with historical personages. The Serbian bard could hardly envisage a poem unconnected with the national tradition.

Of the other historical cycles, the finest deals with the rising against the Dahis (the revolted leaders of the janissaries) in 1804 and the liberation of Serbia under Karageorge. Yet another, to which I have already referred, deals with the exploits of the Uskoks. Another lesser known cycle deals with the life of Sv. Sava, while perhaps the best known of all, wherein history is inextricably mixed up with fantasy, describes the deeds of Marko Kraljević, legendary hero of the Serbs.

Legend has wrought a strange transformation in Marko. In actual fact, he was one of the petty princes who carved out a kingdom for himself after the break-up of the Serbian Empire of Tsar Dušan the Mighty. His capital was at Markovgrad, that huge mass of volcanic rock a mile or so outside Prilep. The lovely monastery of the Holy Archangel is still there, perched high up on the mountain-side, and a number of ruined courts and churches on the rock itself and on the plain below. From its spacious balcony one can look down over the rich Pelargonian plain to Bitola and the heights of Perister. On the doorway of the monastery church can still be seen contemporary portraits of Marko and his father Vukašin, grave, bearded warriors with the eyes of dreaming eagles.

In history, Marko was a vassal of the Turks, and died fighting in the Turkish ranks as an ally. Legend tells us how he prayed, none the less, that the Christians might conquer, though he himself be the first to fall. But it appears that he fought honourably for his overlord. However, the marvellous cycle of the heroic ballads associated with his name has given him a different character. In them he appears more than life size, a hero *sans peur et sans reproche,* at least according to the ideas of his age.

'His *samur kalpak* is pulled low over his dark eyes; his huge black moustache is as large as a lamb of three months' growth; his cloak is a shaggy wolf-pelt; at his girdle swings a damascened blade; on his back is slung a war-spear; at his saddle-bow hangs a mighty mace, with a well-filled wineskin to hold the balance should the saddle slip.'

With his great studded mace and mounted on his wonder horse, Šarac, which drinks the red wine with him – 'half he drank and half to Šarac gave' – he is a figure of fear to the evildoer, whom later ages identified with the Turk. He is not afraid to face the sultan himself, and he ploughs the highways to prevent the Turkish soldiers and merchants from passing.

In the course of the ages he became the hero of the Serbs, a far clearer figure to the peasants than their kings or even the Emperor Dušan himself. He is befriended by the vilas (fairies) of the mountains, and the greatest champions of Islam cannot stand against him. He gradually assumes more and more the character of a hajduk – one of those fierce outlaws, half brigand and half patriot, who kept alive the spirit of rebellion under Turkish rule. He is rough and passionate and cruel, but he never forgets his devotion to Serbia and the Holy Cross. He is the embodiment of the fierce spirit of patriotic revolt, even as the holy Tsar Lazar is the embodiment of a mysticism based on hope. His deeds and his songs have filled the centuries and fill them still. When the satirist Radoje Domanović wished to castigate the vices of his age (just before the war), he could do no better than tell the story of 'Marko Kraljević a second time on earth'.

Such is the Marko of legend. These songs, which have immortalized him, are the greatest heritage of the Yugoslav race. Originating in south Serbia, they are sung throughout all the South Slav lands, even in Bulgaria. The cycle of Marko Kraljević, violent and passionate, was perhaps the favourite of the Middle Ages. Today it seems farther away from us than the lovely cycle of Kosovo.

With the legend of Sv. Sava we come directly into contact with the Serbian monasteries, the second great heritage of the centuries. Here history predominates over legend – perhaps the local priests saw to that – and the main outlines of the story are confirmed by history and the writers of the žitije (lives of the Serbian saints). Sava was the second son of the Grand Župan Nemanja, the founder of the dynasty. His secular name was Rastko. But, even as a young man, court life did not attract him. When only seventeen he fled from court with some wandering monks of the Holy Mountain. When the hue and cry finally found him, he had already shaved his head and taken the monastic vows as the monk Sava. All that his pursuers could bring back to his father were the golden locks that he had cut off and discarded for ever.

For twenty years he resided on the Holy Mountain, where he soon acquired a reputation not only for piety but for reliability and devotion to the interests of the Church. He was soon entrusted with important duties and negotiations between the monks of Athos and the Patriarchs of Constantinople. These duties schooled him in statecraft, which was to prove of inestimable value to him in later years.

But Sava was not only a monk; he was also a Nemanja. He saw clearly that a Serbian national state could only be built up on a Serbian national church. He saw the decadence of Byzantine life and its influence on his young and impressionable people. Yet he respected the civilization of the Greeks and wished the Serbs to get the best from it.

In 1197 his father abdicated and came also to the Holy Mountain, as the monk Simeon. There he built the magnificent monastery of Hilendar, which was for ages the centre of Serbian monastic life. There it was that Sava wrote the life of his father, Stefan Nemanja, in a beautiful clear style that entitles him to be called the first great Serbian writer.

In 1204 his father died and, his restraining influence gone, violent quarrels broke out in Serbia over the succession. Sava left Mt. Athos and returned to his country. Now his training in statecraft served him well. Hungary and Byzantium, both fishing in troubled waters, took different sides in the quarrel. It seemed as if the Serbian state was to fall to pieces a few years after it had been founded. Sava composed the quarrels and ensured the succession.

But in the meantime his opportunity had come, and from a different source. In 1204 the Latins had taken Constantinople, and the Greek Patriarch was forced to flee to Nicaea. The Serbian Church was therefore cut off from the source of authority and was compelled to rely upon the Archbishop of Ohrid, then the subject of a foreign power. Sava, therefore, went to Nicaea and, urging the danger of Latin Church influence in Serbia and the value of the Serbs as an ally against the Latin Emperor of Constantinople, counselled the creation of an autonomous Serbian Orthodox Church. His request was granted by the Patriarch, and Sava himself became the first Archbishop.

He fixed his centre at the monastery of Žiča, whose blood-red towers still stand magnificently in the wooded valley near Kraljevo (for a time known as Rankovičevo). There he controlled the destinies of the Serbian Church until 1233, when he resigned the power of his pupil Arsenius and set out on a pilgrimage to the Holy Land. But meanwhile he had carried out far-reaching and permanent reforms and closely associated the work of the Church with that of the nation and the dynasty. It may truly be said that the mediaeval Serbian state was created materially by the Nemanja dynasty and spiritually by Sava and the Serbian Orthodox Church.

To the end of his life Sava remained a worker. His many voyages always combined piety and statecraft. The last of them was in connexion with the autonomy of the Bulgarian Church, and it was at Trnovo, the holy city of the Bulgarians, that he died, as the guest of the Bulgarian Tsar Asen, on January 12th, 1235, in the sixty-first year of his life. The Bulgarians also loved and esteemed the life and work of Sv. Sava, and it was only under protest that they allowed King Vladimir to take his body from the great Rila monastery to that of Mileševa, where it remained until Sinan Pasha had it exhumed and burnt on the hill of Vračar in Belgrade in 1595.

All creeds venerated Sava and still venerate him. The Catholic king of Bosnia was crowned on his tomb at Mileševa—an Orthodox monastery – and the Catholic sculptor Ivan Meštrović has placed him among the four Slavonic saints. He has continued to live, too, in the hearts of the people as well as of the priests. Many are the peasant tales, some rather naïve, of his wanderings and miracles. He was, perhaps, the greatest of the Nemanjas.

The day of Sv. Sava is usually chosen as the slava of converts to the Serbian Orthodox Church. The slava is a purely Serbian institution; in the very rare cases when you come across it in other parts of Yugoslavia or in Bulgaria, it means that the area has either been Serbian or has been influenced very greatly by Serbian neighbours. The origin of the custom is obscure, but it is generally regarded as the day when the ancestral tribe was converted to Christianity. It has no connexion whatever with a name-day or a birthday.

It is a time of feasting. There is a complicated and very beautiful slava ritual which is strictly kept in the villages, but in the cities is often more honoured in the breach than in the observance. A village slava usually lasts three days. A peasant family will some-times stint itself throughout the whole year to have a good slava. Everyone, without exception, is welcome to the good cheer, but is is usual for invitations to be offered for the slava supper, the high-light of the feast. Strangers are frequently invited and given a place of honour, for the Serbian peasant is nothing if not hospit-able. If you are invited, accept at once.

Incidentally, the custom is so deeply rooted that I have often been invited to the slava of men who are avowed and convinced communists and who regard any other religious festival with aversion and contempt.

On the days of the greatest slavas, such as Sv. Nikola, there may be very many slavas in a single village. I recollect one Sv. Nikola in the village of Temerin where I was a guest. I went to one slava, where I ate and drank almost to bursting point. I was then invited to another, and not to put in an appearance would have been an insult. I could eat no more, only drink. Another invitation followed – and then another. Finally, I had been the guest of honour at nineteen slavas. As I and my host staggered out of the last in the early hours of the morning, we stumbled into our carriage with the remark: 'Thank heaven the horse is still sober!'

The other great heritage of the Middle Ages to the Serbian people has been their mediaeval monasteries.

There are many hundreds of these monasteries, mainly in Serbia and Macedonia, though there are also a few smaller ones in Montenegro and some in what is now Bulgarian and Albanian territory. Many of them have been damaged or destroyed in the numerous wars and revolutions that have harried these distressful lands; but many of the most beautiful are still almost as lovely as on the day when they were first consecrated.

The Turks, of course, paid little heed to these monuments of a great Christian past, and many of the monasteries remained quasi-deserted for centuries. Others, especially those in the more remote parts of the country, served as hideouts for the hajduks, a role they again resumed for the men of the resistance during the last war. Still others were destroyed. Yet enough remain to show that here was one of the great moments of the quickening of the human spirit.

Between the wars Serbian artists and savants stressed the importance of preserving this precious heritage of art. Caretakers were appointed to those that had been deserted and a certain amount of repair work was undertaken. But, on the whole, little was accomplished. Curiously enough, it has been left to a government avowedly indifferent to religion to care for and maintain the monasteries, not indeed for their original purpose but as memorials to the glory of the Serbian past. More honour to the reverence and delicacy of feeling they have used in carrying out this work.

I have before me as I write two monographs on the Serbian monasteries, one written during the First World War and the other published shortly after the Second. The work that has been done in the interval, and which is still going on, is indeed wonderful, and it has been done with taste and discernment, mainly in the provision of roofs to preserve the frescoes and repairs made whenever possible with the original materials. It is strange to think that before 1917 these buildings and frescoes were almost unknown.

This painstaking and devoted labour has revealed about 200 square metres of thirteenth-century fresco in the still older church of Sv. Kliment at Ohrid. The fresco of Christ before Pilate is a masterpiece of the Serbo-Macedonian school.

The origins of Slav Christianity centre around the Lake of Ohrid in the south-west corner of Macedonia, on the Albanian frontier. Travel to Ohrid was restricted for some time after the war, as it lies in a critical frontier area. But the restrictions have been lifted for some time now and there are excellent bus services from Skopje.

There is an air of timelessness about Lake Ohrid. Surrounded by high mountains on three sides, the northern end opens out into a small marshy plain where at one time water-buffalo wallowed in the shallows and the dolaps (huge water-wheels revolving a chain of buckets) lifted water from the lake to irrigate the fields. Today modern methods have altered this; the water-buffalo, save in the Kosmet, have been replaced by lorries and only a few dolaps can be seen, decaying uselessly on the lakeside. Moslem Struga is on the west, where the river Drim pours out of the lake and the local eels are famous among Belgrade gourmets, and Christian Ohrid is on the east. The eels too may soon become victims of progress. New hydro-electric stations on the Drim – one of them has created the huge artificial lake of Mavrovo – have interfered with their normal breeding habits and experts believe that in two or three years they will have ceased to exist.

Ohrid itself was the principal town on the ancient Via Ignatia from Dyrrachium to Thessalonika and one may well imagine the relief and thankfulness of the early voyager emerging from the grim Albanian or Macedonian gorges upon seeing the clear, sparkling waters of this great upland lake.

Yet another victim of progress is the Ohrid fishing boat, with its strange dug-out shape and huge leeboards. This curious design had not altered materially for two thousand years, but now these archaic boats are being rapidly replaced by modern metal dinghies. On my last visit I could find only two of them, mouldering uselessly near the springs where, according to a famous local folk-song, the peasant girl Biljana used to bleach her linen. But the metal dinghies seem steady enough to fish the lake with safety despite the violent squalls that rush down in winter from the surrounding mountains which, even in high summer, are often snow-covered. Their catch, too, is a link with an even more distant past. The famous lake-trout of Ohrid, I am told by prominent ichthyologists, belong to a group long extinct save in Ohrid, neighbouring Prespa and far-distant Baikal in Siberia. Be that as it may, they make excellent eating, whether fresh or smoked, and have been mentioned by epicures for centuries. The poets of the national epics speak of the despots of Serbia, far to the north in Kruševac, feasting on the fish of Ohrid. After the conquest a courier service was organized to bring them to the table of the sultan in Istanbul.

Ohrid is a city of old houses in the Turkish, or it may well be the

Old houses at Ohrid, Macedonia

Byzantine, manner that lean out across the narrow cobbled streets as if eternally gossiping about the past. On the hill above the city the remains of the tremendous fortress of Tsar Samuel stretches its gaping walls and battered outposts seemingly for leagues. In the central square there is an ancient plane-tree that some years ago sheltered a small coffee-house within its battered trunk; the coffee-house has gone but the plane remains. It seems like a contemporary of the fortress. Everywhere you go there are churches, nearly all of them from between the tenth and fourteenth centuries, some mere empty shells, others with magnificent frescoes. As befits the birthplace of Slav Christianity, there are still, in Ohrid or around the lake, some forty of them. In the days of Tsar Dušan there were said to be more than a hundred.

Ohrid was the home of the saints Kliment and Naum, disciples of the first Slavonic apostles, Cyril and Methodius, and as early as the ninth century became a centre of Slavonic culture and Christianity whose influence extended as far as distant Russia. It was here that the Cyrillic alphabet was created and the first church books written in it.

The oldest and most famous of the Ohrid churches is the basilica of Sv. Sofia, at one time the cathedral of the Archbishops of Ohrid. It was built in the ninth century on the ruins of a pagan temple. In Turkish times it was converted into a mosque, the frescoes covered over, the pulpit changed into a mimbar, and a minaret – now removed – was added. But a good deal of careful restoration has been done and the fine frescoes, cleaned of their chalk covering, are little the worse for their long banishment. They provide an interesting contrast between Byzantine and Serbian art. The oldest were painted by order of the Greek Archbishop Leo between 1025 and 1056. They are the oldest and finest Byzantine frescoes in Yugoslavia, save at Poreč. They still maintain the stiff hieratic poses and conventions of mosaic. But there are also fine sequences painted in the later, more naturalistic, Serbo-Macedonian style of the fourteenth century, including a fine Vision of the Last Judgement.

After the conversion of Sv. Sofia into a mosque, the church of Sv. Kliment became the cathedral. It was built by the Byzantine Emperor Andronicus II, but was much enlarged under Serbian rule seventy years later.

Very recent excavations, made in the summer of 1965 by the Macedonian professor Dimče Koco, have revealed the grave of Sv. Kliment, who died in 916 A.D. The grave, with inscriptions and ikons of the period, was found during work on the church of

Sv. Panteleimon which, after the Turkish invasions, was transformed into the Imaret mosque. Another building discovered nearby during the same excavations was probably a dispensary or a hospital for, according to Kliment's biographer, the saint was a famous healer.

I will not weary the reader with an account of all the churches and monasteries of Ohrid. There are many of them and excellent monographs on their frescoes and ikons are easily available. Ohrid is, in fact, one of the best places to see these frescoes at their finest. The old city has been preserved as a national monument and all new building there must conform to the national style, but outside the walls modern Ohrid stretches along the shore with comfortable hotels and other amenities. This is important, since many of the finest frescoed churches of Serbia and Macedonia are somewhat inaccessible, so that it is difficult to spend more than a few hours at a time to see their glories. In Ohrid there is all the time in the world and plenty of counter-attractions, such as bathing, boating, water-skiing and eating the Ohrid trout, to modify a perhaps too indigestible meal of too much mediaeval painting.

Almost all the churches are now museums, but this has one great advantage. The preservation of the frescoes has been done with taste and skill. The accretions of later centuries have been painstakingly removed and the frescoes blaze on the walls with all their original brilliance. The whole gospel story is told there, frequently with subjects rarely to be seen in the West such as the Dormition of the Virgin – a favourite theme, but rare in Western churches – the Mocking of Christ and many legends of the Orthodox saints.

Equally careful has been the restoration of the buildings themselves. One of the most dramatic (though the frescoes are practically non-existent) is that of Sv. Jovan Bogoslov, probably built during the reign of Tsar Dušan, on a rocky cliff overhanging the lake near the fishing village of Kaneo, almost a part of the city of Ohrid itself. It is usually known as Sv. Jovan Kaneo. Here the later buildings have been removed and the church now stands in its original form, a gem of Macedonian-Byzantine architecture, with its dramatic terraces on the cliff edge. When the sun sets over the Albanian mountains to the west, Sv. Jovan Kaneo is a magnificent sight, its rose-red weathered brick shining like a ruby.

Another striking church is Sv. Zaum, a tiny building on the lakeside about half-way to the more famous monastery of Sv. Naum and not far from the picturesque village of Peštani where the beach is covered with fishing nets and the washing of the local peasant woman spread out to dry on the pebbly strand. It is one of the few places where the highly-coloured Macedonian national dress can still frequently be seen. But Sv. Zaum is almost inaccessible from the road; it is better to go by boat.

Most beautiful of all is Sv. Naum on another cliff, at the far end of the lake thirty kilometres away. Here too later buildings have mostly been cleared away, and the church now stands in its original purity. The frescoes, though quaint, are fairly recent but have a naïve charm of their own. They cannot be compared in beauty or interest with those of the Ohrid churches, but personally I like them. In the church itself and over the gateway into the monastery close is a very simple little picture of one of the miracles of Sv. Naum. A local peasant complained to the saint that one of his oxen had been eaten by a bear. The saint reproved the bear and ordered it to take the place of its victim, and the picture shows the peasant driving ox and bear in amicable tandem.

Sv. Naum is a lovely place to visit. Apart from the interest of the old church, the cradle of Slav Christianity, there are the lovely water-meadows around the source of the Black Drim, only a stone's throw from the monastery. There is too a pleasant beach on the lake-shore from which one may have the doubtful and dangerous pleasure of swimming into Albania.

These older foundations were for the most part poor. They could not afford to use mosaic or to pay for the skilled craftsmen necessary to install it who did not relish long trips into these distant provinces. They relied on fresco and carved woodwork, thereby inaugurating a development that came to full fruition in the fourteenth and fifteenth centuries. Most of these artists were anonymous, as was the custom of the times, but now and again one finds a name on a portrait, whether on some subsidiary figure in one of the great frescoes or intertwined in the complicated carving of portal, window or ikonostas. For the most part, these early churches were of brick, often set in complicated designs to afford decoration to cupola or façade.

The Slav states of those early days were transient and amorphous. It was not until the end of the tenth century that two well-defined states arose. These were the Serb state of Zeta, covering what is roughly today Montenegro and the Sanjak, and the Slavo-Macedonian empire of Tsar Samuel, which covered a far wider area and was a serious rival to the Byzantine empire.

With the growing stability of power, the influence of Ohrid began to extend. Churches and monasteries were built, and the lessons of the Gospel, now written in the new and more comprehensible Cyrillic, were read, even if not always obeyed. But of this early period few traces remain, and these mostly in churches that were so completely rebuilt in the times of the Nemanjas that little save the name remains of the earlier foundation.

A visit to the lake of Prespa is well worth-while. It lies even higher in the mountains than Ohrid, with which it is supposed to be connected by underground channels, and it is shallower. There are few settlements around it, and for that very reason it is wilder and its shallow waters and reedy poljes are a paradise of wild life and wild flowers. I can remember visiting Prespa at a time when the narcissi and jonquils were out. The whole polje between Resan and the lake was one unbroken sea of aromatic colour.

But to return to our monasteries. Of those remaining from the eleventh and early twelfth centuries the most interesting is Nerezi, a short walk from Skopje. By a short walk I mean from two to three hours, for the Macedonians are good walkers, and if you ask a peasant how far it is to any given place he is more likely to give you the answer in time than in distance. It is best done very early in the morning, while it is still fresh and when you will meet on the way the peasants coming into Skopje with loads of fruit and vegetables. Later in the day the sun is very hot, and often the only wayfarers you will meet will be the ubiquitous Macedonian tortoises.

The monastery is dedicated to Sv. Panteleimon and was built in 1164, probably by Macedonian masons, for the Byzantine governor of that time, Alexis Comnenos. I see from a recent photograph that a good deal of repair work has been done and the wonderful marble ikonostas that I last saw in fragments has been restored. The frescoes are of various dates. Some, near the altar, are the work of Greek painters, while many of the others have been added by Slav artists. The name of one of them, Stojka, has been preserved.

The empire of Samuel disintegrated after his death, which accounts for the presence of a Byzantine governor in Skopje in 1164. But Serbian power and artistic awakening grew stronger side by side. The founder of the Nemanja dynasty, the Great Župan Stefan Nemanja, was born in Ribnica, now Titograd, in 1164, the year of Nerezi's foundation. His father had been expelled from Raška as the result of some dynastic quarrel.

On his return to Raška, Nemanja organized a state that was to become a kingdom and finally, under Dušan the Mighty, formally an empire. At the height of its power it extended over most of Serbia, all Montenegro, parts of Albania and Bulgaria, and all Macedonia to the gates of Salonica.

With the Nemanjas came their architecture. There is very little point in trying to trace the dynastic history of the Nemanjas. For one thing, it is extremely complicated, and for another, there were sometimes several Serbian states under members of the dynasty at the same time, which makes it very hard to establish a regular sequence in the mind. Also, as frequently with the Slav states of the Middle Ages, their frontiers were extremely fluid and the capital was where the ruler resided, and he often changed his residence.

However, in the two and a half centuries of their power, to the death of Dušan in 1355, Serbia became the most powerful nation of the Balkans, and with its growing power awoke an artistic renaissance that even after the dissolution of the dynasty continued to flourish until the coming of the Turks.

Nor is it possible accurately to divide the architecture of the Nemanjas into 'schools' without so many exceptions that the classification becomes meaningless. It is simplest to divide them geographically and more or less chronologically into the Raška group, the Macedonian group and the Morava group. The last two overlap considerably.

The architects of these wonderful buildings were for the most part anonymous, as were most of the fresco painters. Two only are known to us: Vid of Kotor, who built Dečani, and Rade

Borović, who built several of the fourteenth-century masterpieces of the Morava group.

After Sv. Sava had emerged from his monastic retirement at Hilendar on Mount Athos, he fixed his seat as first Serbian Archbishop at Žiča, in a wooded valley near Kraljevo, once known as Rankovićevo. Its blood-red towers are colour-washed in the manner of the Holy Mountain and are a most extraordinary sight when one first sees them. Žiča was long the coronation church of the Nemanja dynasty and is still known as 'the seven-gated', since for each coronation a fresh entrance was made in the surrounding walls.

The three greatest surviving masterpieces of the Raška group are Studenica, Visoki Dečani and Gračanica. Two other great churches – Djurdjevi Stubovi and Gradac, perhaps once equally beautiful – are in ruins.

In the Raška group, two tendencies are evident. Marble and stone now replace the earlier brick, and the simple decoration of the earlier churches is replaced by doors and windows intricately carved with luxuriant designs of birds, beasts and flowers. Also, in the larger churches, walls, vaults and pillars are all covered with fresco, giving an extraordinary richness to the interiors.

The combination of Byzantine and Western influences has now produced a new style, rich and harmonious, unique in architecture. The frescoes, too, show an amazing advance in subject and technique. The hieratic stiffness of the Byzantine tradition, founded on mosaic, is replaced by an originality of design and freedom of technique that, to my mind, excel the contemporary Italian masters. It is a fascinating theory, for which there is much evidence, that had it not been for the factions following the death of Dušan and the subsequent Turkish conquest the genius of Byzantium would have flowered first in Serbia, and not in Italy, and the glories of the Renaissance would first have blossomed in this land condemned by history to five centuries of servitude.

Incidentally, some of the most lovely of these frescoes and those that support this theory in the most lively fashion are in the half-ruined church at Sopoćani, near Novi Pazar. Since the First World War a roof has been added and the frescoes preserved from the wear and tear of the elements to which they were exposed for hundreds of years. It is a tribute to the technique of the early painters that they have survived.

The white marble church of Studenica in the Ibar valley was built for the Great Župan Stefan Nemanja himself in 1183. It was the first and greatest of the 'royal monasteries' and had a certain autonomy, owing direct allegiance to the king. Its iguman had precedence over the other abbots and held the title of Grand Archimandrite, presiding over the council that elected the Patriarch.

Not only in its material does Studenica show influences of the Dalmatian masons who brought with them the ideas of the West. The details of doors and windows are more Romanesque than Byzantine, and the lions upon which the pillars of the main door-way rest recall the later ones of Šibenik. Several of the original twelfth-century frescoes have remained intact, including a fine portrait of Sv. Sava. Others have been restored with care and reverence, so that the church as a whole has retained its artistic unity. The frescoes were added, after Nemanja's death, by his son Vukašin who, with many others of the Nemanja dynasty, is buried here.

High Dečani is perhaps the most lovely of all the monasteries. Some of its unique beauty is due to the harmony of its proportions, but even more to its material, courses of reddish, steel-blue and grey marble, which have mellowed to a lovely gradation of tone. Dečani is easily reached by road from Peć and lies in a fold of the mountains just off the fertile valley of the Metohija in a forest of flowering chestnuts, watered by one of the many streams with the name of Bistrica (the swift one). It was commenced in 1327 by Stefan Uroš III, who is therefore usually known as Dečanski, and completed by his son, Dušan the Mighty, in 1335, who also added the frescoes thirteen years later.

The fact that it was built by a Catholic – the Franciscan friar, Vid of Kotor – is a striking tribute to the religious tolerance and national unity of those days. The interior is frescoed throughout. There are more than a thousand of them, covering every detail of the church, even the pillars, whence various Stylite saints and a grave bearded Christ look down on one. A whole wall is decorated with the family tree of the Nemanjas, where every face has life and character. It is the most beautiful of the Serbian monasteries, less austere but more human than Mileševa, a fairyland of colour where every picture is connected either with Holy Writ or with the Serbian past.

Architecturally the most interesting of the Raška churches is Gračanica on the Field of Kosovo. It was a foundation of King Milutin and his unfortunate child-wife, Simonida, in 1321. The church is five-cupolaed, of finely polished stone. The frescoes have been considerably damaged, but are still beautiful. Amongst them is a portrait of Simonida, which is the subject of one of the most lovely poems in the Serbian language by Milan Rakić.

The churches and monasteries of Raška developed, little by little, into the more elaborate style of the Morava valley. But in the meantime Serbia had extended southwards, to include the greater part of Macedonia, and Tsar Dušan had been crowned by three Archbishops at Skopje as 'Tsar of the Serbs, Greeks and Albanians'. Men's eyes looked southward. Belgrade was outside the Empire; but there were hopes, not to be realized, that Salonica, and perhaps even Constantinople, the City of the Caesars itself, might shortly be within it.

It is worth pointing out, before going farther, that though the might of the Serbian Empire declined sharply after the death of Dušan, its artistic brilliance continued for nearly another century under his weak son, Uroš the Child, and the various princes, despots and nobles who, under various titles, carved themselves out petty principalities from the decaying corpse of the Empire. Amongst them was Marko Kraljević.

Of the very many churches and monasteries of Macedonia let three serve as examples: Markovgrad, Matejić, Staro Nagoričane.

I have already said something of Markovgrad earlier in this chapter when speaking of Marko himself. On that crowded rock, as well as on the plain below, there are many wonderful old churches, whose beauty you may share with the lizards and the tortoises. One of the most lovely of them is the Church of Sv. Dimitrije, from the time of Marko himself.

Markovgrad is almost entirely deserted. These 'ghost-towns' of the Balkans are strange places to explore, even if they fill the soul with dreams of forgotten grandeur and gloomings about mortality.

There are many of them: Perast, Markovgrad, Melnik in Bulgaria, and, most wonderful of all, Mistra in the Vale of Sparta in Greece. They are the result of the constant shiftings of peoples and of cultures in this much-bedevilled peninsula, where one civilization followed another and did not wish to, or could not, build upon the earlier foundation.

More modern times have also a worthy memorial at Prilep, where the revolutionary movement first broke out in Macedonia. It is called the Tomb of the Unconquered and is bold in conception and modernist in design, the work of the Macedonian sculptor, Jordan Grabulovski. Black and white, rough-hewn marble steps lead to a long line of black marble busts which commemorate the first heroes of the outbreak, almost all of them young men in their twenties. Then, wide stairways lead to the top of the hill where there is a circle with eight irregular and strangely shaped urns in rough white stone. The effect is bizarre but strangely impressive. Behind these, in a sort of roofless cave of highly polished white marble is the roll-call of the victims, a tiny coat-of-arms before the name commemorating those who have been proclaimed national heroes.

The two churches that I have chosen as examples of the Macedonian style are both near Kumanovo. One, Matejić, is on the mountain ridge overlooking the plain; the other, Staro Nagoričane, is to the east of Kumanovo on the plain itself.

I had often seen Matejić from the train between Niš and Skopje as a white flash on the mountain-top at so great a distance I had scarcely been able to distinguish it. One day I determined to visit it.

I did so in a fiacre that lumbered slowly across the Kumanovo plain towards the village of Matejić at the foot of the mountains. My driver was an old soldier, who chatted to me about the great Serbian victory here in the Balkan wars. For Kumanovo and Kosovo are the battlefields of the Balkans. Whoever controls Kumanovo controls the Vardar and Morava river valleys, the ancient invasion route, either southward to Salonica or northward through the Morava valley to the Danube. The headwaters of the two rivers approach one another at this point, and some far-sighted dreamers have even conceived a scheme to link the Aegean and the Danube by canals.

I stopped at the village for information and rakija. The monastery, they said, was about two hours' walk. Luckily I had had experience of Macedonian ideas of distance and insisted that my driver took me at least part of the way up. We toiled on for another four hours, along a rough road serpentining the curves of the mountain, with the cupolas of the church always getting deceptively a little nearer. At last I told my driver to stop and give the horses a breather; I would walk the rest. Even so, it took me another full hour.

Matejić, the Church of the Virgin of the Black Mountain, is a magnificent five-cupolaed building of the best period of Serbo-Macedonian architecture. The frescoes are good but much damaged, and that of the donor which is usually to be found just inside the main portal is so damaged as to be unrecognizable. But there are records of the monastery as early as 1300 and it was probably built in the reign of Milutin, between 1282 and 1321, though the frescoes are some half-century later.

It was one of the 'royal monasteries' and was at one time very rich. It had extensive buildings and guest-rooms, a school for the daughters of the nobility, and a special chapel for the Imperial family. King Milutin is said to have been crowned there, and Jelena, the sister of Tsar Dušan the Mighty, was its benefactress. Her portrait in the stiff, formal robes of the Imperial Court is still to be seen among the much-damaged frescoes. It was she who repaired the church in the fourteenth century after it had been damaged by an earthquake.

At the time when I visited Matejić the support wall on the mountain edge had fallen away, and with it a part of the chapel wall, so that poor sightless Jelena looked out over hundreds of miles of the wide plain of Kumanovo that once she had helped to rule.

Sightless, because the eyes and faces of the saints – and few could distinguish between the saints and the members of the imperial family – had long been picked away by pious and ignorant peasant women, who believe that this hallowed dust will help them to bear children.

The church has now been restored, many of the ramshackle monastery buildings removed and the *zareba* of thorn bushes that encircled it at the time of my visit has been cleared away. It is no longer melancholy but proud and defiant in its magnificent position on the mountain top. It was only in the ages of faith that men sought to build in such an inaccessible spot.

Much too has been done to preserve what is left of the frescoes, though one of the most interesting of them – a family tree of the Byzantine emperors – is so damaged as to be almost incomprehensible. It is certainly tiring to visit Matejić, but it is equally certainly rewarding.

Staro Nagoričane is more easily approached. It lies in the plain to the east of Kumanovo, and the road is easily found, firstly because it is the only one and secondly because a huge memorial to the victory at Kumanovo marks the way.

Nagoričane was obviously at one time another of those very important cities on the Morava–Vardar route. It lies at the crossways of the two most important roads. The church of St George is very ancient. It was probably built in Byzantine times and is attributed to the Emperor Romanus Diogenes, but an inscription of Tsar Samuel would place some foundation on the site in even earlier times. But the present church was entirely rebuilt in the time of the Nemanjas by Milutin, the same king who built Matejić. Its frescoes are wonderful, though somewhat damaged by Bulgarian troops who occupied the church in the Balkan wars and scribbled upon the walls up to arms' length. Above that they are in good condition.

Mlado (young) Nagoričane is within a minute or two on foot. Here are the remains of some twelve churches of the Middle Ages, all of interest, but in a sad condition. In one of them a modern restorer has been at work. The result is interesting but horrible. Thank goodness he had either the reverence or the cowardice not to attempt to improve on the Church of St George.

If I were to speak of all the churches and monasteries of Macedonia it would require a whole book – a very interesting one, to be sure, but not the one I am now writing. I will mention but one more: the tiny church of Sv. Andrea in the Treska gorge. It is very small, with scarcely room inside for more than a priest and a congregation of half a dozen. It was built in 1388, in a tremendous gorge which was at one time approachable only by water; on the other side of the gorge are the remains of a mediaeval convent which I have never discovered how to approach. But now the Treska gorge has been turned into the Skopje water supply and the former torrent turned into a lake.

A path has been cut in the rock-wall, so Andrea is today easily reached. Also there is a comfortable kafana there, with boats. But one must take care to get the key to the tiny monastery before leaving Skopje, for it is being repaired and kept closed. Sv. Andrea is well worth a visit, the more so as ancient Macedonia may comfortably be compared with the more modern and practical achievements of modern Yugoslavia. The dam is a fine one, the power-station suitably unobtrusive, and the view magnificent.

Incidentally the frescoes of Sv. Andrea are also worth seeing. The church being so small, they are hard to see without an electric torch, and at one time in the history of the church an Albanian has had a cut at some of them with an axe, but none the less they are worthy of respect.

As the Turks pressed northwards, eating up one by one the petty Macedonian principalities, what remained of the Serbian power was concentrated in the north and centre of the country, more especially in the Morava valley. Serbia was still a wealthy state, though a weak one, even after Kosovo and the despots (the Imperial title had lapsed) drew their wealth from the silvermines of Novo Brdo.

This period was the last flowering of the Serbian architectural genius, and is closely associated with the name of the great architect Rade Borović.

The churches of this period borrow from Eastern models, but preserve the monumental form and to some extent the materials of the Raška group. The architectural form becomes more complicated, a particularly striking innovation being the increased height of the cupola and the decorative use of the belfry. The outer decoration becomes far more elaborate, so that in churches like Kalenić (early fifteenth century) it looks almost like sculptured lace. The frescoes are still in the grand style.

The great churches of this group include Ravanica (1381, and not to be confused with another Ravanica in the Fruška Gora), Lazarica (also c. 1380) and Resava (early fifteenth century),

Window of the monastery-church of Kalenić (XV century)

usually known simply as Manasija (the monastery).

Resava was a foundation of one of the last despots, Stefan Lazarević Visoki (The Tall). The colossal stone walls which surround it are an indication of the troublous times in which it was built. As at Smederevo, they are modelled on the Long Walls of Constantinople.

The fall of Smederevo marked the end of Serbia. It is true that some churches and monasteries were built in the early days of Turkish rule, but they are small and without architectural pretensions, a mere shadow of what had been before. Also, there was no more great fresco-painting. Now and again some local painter would try to restore some of the damaged frescoes of earlier ages, but the result is more quaint than magnificent. Curiously enough, it is only now that one occasionally finds external frescoes, which are uncommon in Serbia, though there are fine examples in Rumania, often by Serb painters. These little churches were usually in very isolated spots, as in the towns no Christian church was allowed to overlook a Moslem dwelling, with the result that some, as Sv. Spas at Skopje, are built almost underground. Fresco-painting was almost dead, but strangely enough the art of wood-carving continued and flourished with the masters of the Debar school, some of whose best work dates from the seventeenth and eighteenth centuries.

The work of the Church was now to keep itself and the national tradition alive. It could no longer create, but only preserve. But there was one more quickening of the creative spirit after the Great Migrations into what was then Austrian territory north of the Danube. In the pleasant hill-country of the Fruška Gora, north of Belgrade, there are still a dozen or more Serbian Orthodox monasteries. Very lovely they are, set among orchards and fertile fields. But their architecture and their painting – for frescoes they have none – are so strongly influenced by the Austrian baroque that they have almost·ceased to represent Serbia. Their task, too, was to preserve. To create was beyond their powers.

A beautiful modern example of Serbian church architecture is the church at Oplenac in the heart of a wine-growing district in the smiling Šumadija. It is the zadužbina of King Peter I Karageorgević. A zadužbina is a personal bequest to the church and in most cases the donor is pictured just within the main entrance offering a model of the church he has built to the saint to whom it is dedicated.

Under Turkish rule the peasants lived in their village zadrugas, or family organizations (the word today merely means a co-operative), more or less ignored, save for the visits of tax collectors. They became backward and ignorant; literature, art and education practically did not exist. But national tradition lived fiercely, upheld by the Church, sustained by the national customs and given colour and life by the marvellous oral literature of the heroic ballads. When the time came for revolt, the peasants of the Šumadija knew why.

King Peter chose Oplenac as the site for his great church because of its close association with the first Serbian insurrection, led by his ancestor Black George Petrović, founder of the dynasty. It was at the village of Orašac, near Topola, that the Serbian leaders, driven to extremes by the oppression of the Turks, met secretly and determined at least to die fighting. It was at Topola itself that the standard of revolt was raised and Karageorge chosen as the leader. Topola is the nearest village to the hill of Oplenac, on which the church stands.

Karageorge had lived on and off at Topola for twenty years before the insurrection as a pig-breeder, pigs being then, as now, one of the principal sources of wealth in the Serbian villages. He had also served under the Austrians, where he had learnt something of the military technique of that time – knowledge that served him in good stead in later years.

The career of Karageorge, begun in glory, ended in tragedy. Forced to leave the country, he took no part in the second insurrection under Prince Miloš Obrenović, who obtained a measure of self-government, partly by arms, partly by skilful diplomacy. Karageorge, meanwhile, was in touch with the Hetairia, which dreamed of a Balkan federation of free states, and he returned to Serbia determined to try to win complete freedom by force of arms. He landed at Smederevo and made his presence known there to Voevod Vuličević, who advised Miloš. Miloš felt that Karageorge's plan would endanger both the newly acquired position of the Serbs and his own personal position. Karageorge was killed secretly in his tent, and his head sent to the pasha of Belgrade, who sent it to Sultan Mahmud II.

It is difficult to blame Miloš for his action. Turkey was again strong and it was time for diplomacy rather than open conflict. So far, his action was that of a statesman. But it is certain that Miloš was actuated by personal motives and love of a power which he would not share with another, especially with one so powerful and so beloved as Karageorge. But the worst result of his action was to commence a terrible feud between the Karageorgević and Obrenović dynasties which darkened the whole political history of Serbia in the nineteenth century until it was finally wiped out in blood in 1903.

Now that the Karageorgević dynasty has also gone, it is easier to try to assess who was right and who was wrong. Easier, yes – but of little profit.

However, the great church remains. It was finished in 1912, and its style develops naturally from the mediaeval tradition. It is especially beautiful in winter, when the country is covered with snow; the trees form lovely frosted traceries around the white marble church, and the bright colours of the mosaics – for the traditional frescoes have been copied in mosaic – show even more brilliantly in the hard, white snow-glare.

The church is marble throughout. The altars, the columns and the choir-stalls are of white marble, there is a band of green marble 6 feet broad around the church, and the floor is also in marble of various shades of grey and yellow. Its austerity is tempered by the brilliance of the mosaics, which are said to be made up of more than fifteen thousand shades. It is probably the finest piece of modern mosaic work in existence, only rivalled by the wonderful council chamber of the Stockholm Town Hall.

Albanians from the Kos-Met region

CHAPTER XII

The Federal Capitals

Belgrade revived – A city of gourmets – Serbian wines and Danube fish –
The Kalemegdan – Background to Belgrade – Zagreb and the Croats – The
Peasants' Revolt and Matija Gubec – Ljubljana – The Slovene temperament
– Earthquake at Skopje.

The division of the country into Federal Republics is one of the
principal achievements of the present regime. There are six of
them, and two autonomous areas. Some such form of federalism
was eagerly sought for and demanded even before the war, but
over-centralization, apathy, local jealousies and vested interests
prevented its coming into force until it was too late to have any
effect. It was a valuable reform, for it corresponds to reality.

The jealousies still exist, but they are modified by local government and are no longer the burning problem that they once were.

It is upon the federal capitals, more especially Belgrade, Zagreb
and Ljubljana, that the somewhat experimental legislation of the
new regime has borne most hardly. But it is no part of my purpose
in this book to discuss politics and policy. I shall merely record
their impact on the cities themselves.

Nor do I want to indulge in that nostalgia for things past which
is the sign either of advancing age or of an *émigré* mentality. One
can easily sympathize with those who regret the passing of, say,
Imperial Vienna, Edwardian London or Tsarist Petrograd. But
those cities have passed in spirit, though they still exist materially.
Progress does not necessarily mean pleasure or comfort. Values
change, and it is indeed a hard world for those who are unable to
change with them.

Shortly after the war Belgrade in particular was in the doldrums.
The pre-war gaiety of the city, which was its chief attraction, had
disappeared, the typical kafana life was almost non-existent,

foodstuffs and consumer goods were scarce, poor in quality and bureaucratically controlled.

But a great deal has taken place since then. The spontaneous gaiety which is the charm of the people of Belgrade has returned. Personal fears and excess of bureaucracy still remain, but less oppressively, and are perhaps not evident to the average visitor. The friendliness and hospitality of the people are still evident.

Despite the many changes that have taken place in Belgrade since the terrible days of the war, the principal charm of the city still lies in its people. For, except for its magnificent situation at the confluence of the Sava and the Danube, it is rather a nondescript city. I was there during the German air attacks of April 1941, when much of the old Belgrade that I knew went up in fire and smoke. When I left my flat that day not only was my own house burning, but whole streets were filled with flaming incendiaries and coils of broken telephone wire.

The result has been that whole areas of the comfortable but rather shabby pre-war Belgrade have vanished, the public squares have become larger by devastation, and many old landmarks have disappeared altogether. Extensive post-war planning has also left its mark.

Belgrade with its outer suburbs is now fast approaching the million mark. Most of the development is across the Sava and along the Danube bank, almost engulfing the old city of Zemun. The way in to the centre of the city from the airport is through new Belgrade, a vast agglomeration of apartment houses. Much of this is still being built so that it is not fair to judge it as it is, but better to use the eye of faith to see it as it will be. There has not been time for trees to grow and provide not only beauty but also much-needed shade, while the parks and gardens reveal only a tentative layout. But there is a touch of solidity, even magnificence, about the river-front seen across the Danube from the terraces of the Kalemegdan. These new skyscrapers appear to be solid and well-built, but they have been constructed with a haste which does not inspire too great confidence. In one such modern apartment house (to be fair, not in Belgrade) a guest laughing heartily at a joke leant so heavily on the wall of the sitting room that he fell through it into the bathroom.

The old Terazije in the centre of the city – the word does not mean 'terraces' but 'weighing-scales' for it was once the Turkish octroi – has been modernized. The result is grander, but I for one regret the central fountain with its little tortoises whose whitened backs added a touch of fantasy on snowy days.

Belgrade, too, has suffered heavily from the post-war vice of political nomenclature. The street in which I used to live had four different names within a decade. But, to speak quite fairly, that is not entirely a post-war vice. Old citizens of Belgrade will still direct the visitor by old familiar street-names long out of use. For example, Mackenzieva Street, named after a Scottish reformist preacher whose chapel on the Slavija square has long since been a cinema. The name passed out of official use somewhere about 1914.

Belgrade is used to destruction. In its long history it has been sacked or destroyed more than a score of times. It is little wonder that it is nondescript, with the rebuilding of one destruction over-lying the remnants of many earlier cities. But, none the less, it is a city with the virtues and vices of youth, now perhaps more notice-able than ever before. It is energetic and hasty, inconsiderate and careless of consequence – consider the *coup d'état* of March 1941. It has moments of rare beauty, tempered by others of the sheerest vulgarity. It has grandiose plans, which are often spoilt by mediocre achievement. So it is always tearing down to begin anew. It has an enormous tolerance – less marked since the war – for all that does not get directly in its way; then it has moments of pure fanaticism. Its people have a love of wine, women and song which is often a crust concealing a spiritual shyness and a tre-mendous sense of the ideal. But at least it is alive!

It is a city of the most violent contrasts, as befits its position as key to West and East. In it are many sensitive and cultured artists, but its public artistic life is contemptible. Socially, it varies from almost harem-like restrictions to an ultra-modern freedom, the latter increased and the former restricted by the terrible housing shortage after the war. Amours are everywhere, but there is little or no organized vice. It has almost no nightlife in the Western sense of the world – such as it has is merely a bad copy – but in few other cities does one so often sit until dawn with wine and song. It bristles with rumours and intrigues – known to the initiates as Radio Mileva, after a dancing puppet that used to go the rounds of the kafanas – but no one takes these very seriously. There is little grey in the life of Belgrade, but there is a bewildering cross-cross of black and white.

Belgrade, too, is a city of gourmets. The Serbian cuisine is excellent and has recovered from the shortages and substitutes of war and political repression.

The local reputation of the kafanas is always rising or falling, according to the quality of the wine or the capacity of the cook. Any resident will be able to tell you which is currently in vogue. A good working rule is that music often goes with good wine, but seldom with good food. Eat peaceably and in silence, and then listen elsewhere to the singers, with black coffee and good wine.

I have earlier spoken extensively about the Serbian cuisine. But there are one or two delicacies peculiar to Belgrade and Central Serbia which should be added to that disquisition. Try pršuta – dried meat cut in very thin slices, so that the light shining through them shows a dark red. The best is from pork and is made at Užice; that from beef is not to be recommended for the un-initiated. There is good black caviare from Kladovo – authentic sturgeon this (I once helped to catch a 500-pounder in the whirl-pools below the Iron Gates) – and not so good, but cheaper, red caviare from Ohrid, coming from the lake-trout. A young Danube sterlet – kečiga – cooked on the grill is the most delicious of all fresh-water fish. A thing to remember is that the kečiga has no bones save the horny carapace of its snout and face. The som, or giant Danube catfish, is a fatty fish that needs careful cooking. When young, however, it can be excellent. Approach it with care and good advice.

There are excellent local wines from the Fruška Gora or Smede-revo vineyards and some also from the former royal vineyards around Oplenac. The white varieties are good without being especially distinguished. Good red wine comes from the Župa, Prokuplje, Negotin and Smederevo. The heaviest is the Negotin, a little rough in flavour, but excellent with grills. Prokupac is a medium heavy type of original flavour. A good rosé is the Smederev-ska Ružica, made from the sweetish aromatic Homburg grape. It has a slight muscatel flavour. A drier ružica comes from the Župa.

The wines of Macedonia are a post-war development. On my way south I visited the Tikveš winery at Kavadarci. It is one of many, though one of the largest, and this year (1965) expects to increase its output to eighty wagons a day. The good-humoured director insisted that I taste all his wines and later presented me with a case to continue the experiment. There are too many varieties to be mentioned here, but of the white my personal taste was for the Žilavka (named after the famous Hercegovinian wine) and the Pinogris, of the red the Kavadarka and the Kratošija. Many of these Macedonian wines are obtainable in England.

The glory of Belgrade is the Kalemegdan. The old Kalemegdan fortress is on a high bluff overlooking the confluence of the Danube and the Sava. It has for centuries been regarded as the key to the Balkans and is a natural centre of communications.

From its terraces one looks out over a countryside that changes with the seasons in a cycle of ever-familiar novelty. During the spring floods there is nothing but a sheet of dirty brown water with limits hinted rather than defined by the drowned tree-tops of the islands and the farther bank. Out of this desolate mass rise a few fisherman's huts, various navigation marks and the pathetic and deserted pavilions of the bathing establishments. As the floods subside, leaving behind them a rich coating of silt, the banks and islands begin to assume a definite shape, and break into the green of willows, marsh-forest and tangles of matted briars with an almost ferocious exuberance. By summer the banks and islands rise high out of the water and are covered by the allotments of market-gardeners, yellow with squashes and canteloups, dark-green with the firm, shiny bulks of the water-melons and uncertainly red with ripening tomatoes. Backwaters and mosquito-haunted pools are covered in water-lilies, and the river steamers, searching for deeper channels, make unexpected detours. The usual red-brown melancholy of autumn and the bitter winds and ice-bound shallows of winter complete the accustomed cycle.

The rivers here form a natural boundary. Not necessarily a political one. For centuries one empire or another has held both river-banks: Romans, Byzantines, Serbs, Hungarians, Turks, Austrians, and now again the Serbs. But it is the boundary between the hills and the plain, a boundary which has been strong enough to exert its peculiar influence on all its conquerors and to divide in spirit not only men of the same race but even of the same family. The average Englishman who looks vaguely at the map of southern Europe and calls all the land north of the Danube and Sava 'Central Europe' and all south of it 'the Balkans' is wrong historically, ethnographically and politically. But he is right socially. This human frontier has been blurred from time to time. There has always been a lively and vigorous interchange of men and ideas from one side to the other of the rivers. But broadly speaking it has been a frontier that is, and always will be, maintained. Geography has seen to that!

Needless to say, such a site has been inhabited from the very earliest times. In prehistoric days there were settlements here, as also at Zemun and Pančevo, and at Vinča, a few miles down the Danube. There were communications between them and the pre-Greek civilizations of the Aegean, but they were evidently later broken, as in neolithic times the Danube cultures were purely Central European.

For a time the Illyrians held Belgrade, until displaced by the great migration of the Celts in the fourth century B.C. They lived here more than three hundred years, and called their city Singidunum, by which name it was known to the Romans. The little river on which Pančevo now stands is still called the Tamiš, the same Celtic root as our Thames.

Under the Romans, Belgrade was an important trading centre, but it was never of much administrative importance. The great Roman cities were at Sisak (Siscia), Sremska Mitrovica (Sirmium) and Niš (Naissus). The main legionary camp was at Viminacium, now the insignificant village of Kostolac.

In Byzantine times Belgrade increased in importance and was the seat of an Arian bishop. The Huns demolished it. Justinian the Great rebuilt it. By then it was no longer a commercial and cultural centre, but only a precarious outpost of empire.

In the Dark Ages the list of conquerors grows rapidly; Huns, Avars, Kumans, Bulgarians and many other transient and ephemeral empires won and lost it. The one important fact in all this welter of nameless history is the coming of the Slavs who, though not at once colonizing Belgrade, occupied the country around it and settled there, where they remain to this day.

In the early Middle Ages, Belgrade once more appears upon the scene of definite history. Still a Byzantine frontier city, it was vigorously disputed by the energetic Hungarians, 'a cavalry people with an iron rule', and the growing power of the Serbs. These two peoples, in fact, disputed the possession of Belgrade for over three hundred years.

Belgrade first became a Serbian capital under King Stefan Nemanja the First – crowned in the twelfth century. Though subject to violent attacks by the Hungarians, it was still the capital of Stefan Dragutin Nemanja and was an important city under Stefan Milutin. But the movement of the Serbian power was southward. After the death of Dušan, Belgrade was once again a frontier city and quickly lost.

At the time of the Ottoman invasion, Belgrade was the capital of the Serbian despot, Stefan Lazarević Visoki (The Tall). But his successor, George Branković, was forced to hand it over to the Hungarians, and built as his capital Smederevo, whose mighty ruins can still be seen on the river's edge a few miles down the Danube. Despite the fact that it was seriously damaged by the explosion of an ammunition dump during the war, it is still a most impressive sight.

For nearly three hundred years Belgrade was a Turkish city, and even in the Belgrade of today one can still find traces of their rule. Throughout the seventeenth and eighteenth centuries the forces of Christendom, at last awake to the dangers of Turkish invasion by the conquest first of Serbia then of Hungary and the repeated attacks on Vienna, lay before the walls of Belgrade and pitted their greatest generals against the invader. In 1688 it was taken by Maximilian Emanuel of Baden, but was lost again two years later. In 1717 it was once more taken by Prince Eugene of Savoy, the foremost general of his age, and was held by Austria until 1739. It was at this time that most of the fortifications of the Kalemegdan were built. Their outlines can easily be traced from the upper terraces near Meštrović's statue of the Victor, or from Kaiser Wilhelm's seat, erected pretentiously and bombastically during the First World War.

Today the old fortifications have been turned into pleasant

walks and alleys. There is also an excellent restaurant where one may eat in peace while looking out over the two great rivers. The little church of Ružica also dates from this time, and owes its singular preservation to the fact that the Turks used it as a powder magazine. In the upper park is the tulbe, or tomb, of Mustafa Pasha, the 'Mother of the Serbs', who was killed here by the indignant janissaries, but popular tradition also associates it with that other Mustafa, 'the Black', who tried to take Vienna in 1683.

But it was only by a national movement that Belgrade could be freed once and for all. This came about through Turkish oppression and misrule. In the first years of the ninteenth century the pashaluk of Belgrade was governed by Pasha Mustafa, an enlightened man who protected the Serbs. But the hereditary caste of the janissaries conspired against him, killed him in the Belgrade Kalemegdan and organized a rule of force under their leaders, the Dahis, defying even the sultan himself. Fearing the Serbs, they organized a massacre of their leaders, and the people, driven to extremities, took up arms. They chose as their leader Kara or 'Black' George Petrović, a man of undoubted military genius. He welded the Balkan Serbs into a fighting force which, driven on by the powerful influences of patriotism and despair, was irresistible. Karageorge entered Belgrade in triumph in 1806 and made it his capital.

For those with a knowledge of the Serbian language, the insurrection is marvellously and poetically described in one of the greatest cycles of the national epics and also, with more historical accuracy and almost as much poetry, in the Memoirs of Prota Matija Nenadović, one of the few educated men in Serbia at that time, who became Karageorge's principal diplomatic representative.

The European Powers then took a hand in the game of Balkan politics, which gradually degenerated into the ignoble and intricate chafferings of the Eastern Question, Serbia being used as a pawn to further the ambitions first of Austria and then of Russia. A few years after the revolt of Karageorge, the Turks returned in force, suppressed the revolt and re-entered Belgrade.

Oppression began again, worse than before. For a time the Serbian people, through their spokesman, Miloš Obrenović, tried to obtain concessions from the Porte. At last nothing was left save to embark on a second rebellion. Belgrade again became Serbian, though the Kalemegdan remained in the hands of the Turks. By a hatti-sherif (irrevocable edict) of the sultan, read to the people of Belgrade in 1830, the Serbs obtained a sort of qualified independence.

The position could not last. The new Serbia grew daily more powerful and the Turkish Empire more and more disorganized. Finally, a minor quarrel between Serbs and Turks led to the commandant of the fortress ordering a bombardment of the undefended city. The situation now became critical, and the Turks could no longer maintain their position. Belgrade and the seven other fortresses in Turkish hands were 'confided to the care of Prince Michael'. Turkish pride was saved and the Serbs remained *de facto* masters of their country. On April 6th 1867, Riza Pasha, the last Belgrade Mutasherif, handed over the keys of the fortress to Prince Michael. Belgrade and Serbia were free.

Seventy-four years later, almost to the day, came Hitler's attack on Belgrade, which was eventually liberated once more by the people, this time the whole Yugoslav people, by Tito and his partisans, aided by the Soviet Army. Tito, being still alive, cannot yet be assigned his place in history, though it will certainly be a high one. His life and his career have much in common with those of both Karageorge and Miloš. The comparison is an entertaining essay in historical parallelism. Doubtless when the mists of ideological squabble have subsided he will be placed among their company.

Among the post-war reconstruction projects has been the Belgrade–Zagreb motor-road. It is a fine piece of work. But the journey is a dull one, over the rich but featureless Slavonian plain. It is better to go to Zagreb by train, preferably by night, or by air.

Zagreb suffered far less than Belgrade both during and after the war. Save for the removal of the giant equestrian statue of Ban Jelačić from the central square, a post-war visitor would remark little difference. Incidentally, before the war the main place of rendezvous used to be 'under the tail' of his charger. I wonder what has taken its place.

Zagreb had a few moments of spurious glory during the war,

The Štrosmajer Alley in the old city of Zagreb

as the capital of an 'independent' puppet state. The Croat Ustaša state, born of murder, continued in dishonour and foundered in ridicule, is not a subject that many people in Zagreb will care to discuss. At the height of its excesses, during which some three hundred thousand Orthodox Serbs were murdered and many others subjected to forcible conversion, it represented the boiling point of Serbo-Croatian resentments. The horrified reaction has probably improved them to a point seldom before attained.

The Serbo-Croat rivalries are not a subject for this book, though much could be written on them. They have an ugly, though somewhat comic resemblance to the centuries-old rivalry of English and Irish. They stem from a thousand years of differing historical and cultural tradition, stressed by the difference in religion. Perhaps the most pertinent comment came from a Belgrade pre-war satiric paper, *The Shaven Hedgehog*. At an exhibition of modern French painters then being held in Belgrade, two Serbian peasants were depicted gazing at a Braque cubist picture. One says to the other: 'Just look! Even the French have made a picture of the Croatian problem!'

The modern city of Zagreb is somewhat Austrian in appearance. It has fine workers' quarters, of which it is immensely proud, and a busy city centre around the Republic Square and the main shopping street, the Ilica. The old city is built upon the hill of Grič. There, in front of the Church of St Mark with its gorgeously coloured tiled roof, is the stone upon which Matija Gubec, leader of the peasants' revolt, is said to have suffered for championing the cause of the people against the feudal nobles. He was crowned there with a red-hot crown, seated on a red-hot throne, after tortures unspeakable. One of the church dignitaries assisting is said to have gone mad and to have died, crying out: 'Blood, blood, blood! . . .'

By present-day standards the programme of Matija Gubec was not unreasonable. It boiled down to 'the land for the peasants and the abolition of serfdom'. But for the seventeenth century it was too radical. His men got out of hand and committed excesses, though nothing comparable to those of the nobles against them. His peasant army was soon routed and he himself captured.

Time, however, brings its own revenges. Today Matija Gubec is a national hero, and memorials have been formally unveiled to him by distinguished popular leaders.

A Zagreb professor told me that Matija Gubec was probably not burned here, but before the cathedral. It doesn't matter. Legend has it that he was burned here, and legend is sometimes more important than fact.

It is a very pleasant place, this Upper City. Its palaces are those of the old Croat nobility, and history is in all its stones. The palace of Baron Rauch is now part of the federal republican administration, and I have interviewed a communist Prime Minister here amid scenes of baroque splendour. The noise and bustle of modern Zagreb far below in the Republic Square and along the Ilica, whither one descends by a primitive funicular, are stilled. To get down by car one must take the steep road through the Kamenita Vrata – the Stone Gateway – a favourite shrine, where your vehicle will pass through the smoke of a thousand candles flickering before holy pictures and amidst peasants and townswomen kneeling before the Madonna. Whatever the outcome of the rivalries between the Vatican and the State, they do not affect the simple piety of the Kamenita Vrata.

From the Štrosmajer Alley, named after the greatest of Croat churchmen, one may look out over the modern city of Zagreb below, with its modern hotels and busy, tree-lined squares stretching in well-ordered lines to the open space before the station.

I find it difficult to make up my mind about Zagreb. It is a cultivated city, a proud city, and a capital. Yet there is something provincial about it. It never seems to have been able to break loose from the chains of its own tradition, which for a thousand years was dependent on the foreigner and the whims of a distant Court. In no other large city have I come across such clique bitterness. I had thought this had died out since the war, but that is not true; it is merely less openly expressed. If you ask about some distinguished artist, painter, or writer, nine times out of ten you will get the reply: 'I used to know so-and-so well, a few years ago. But we are not on speaking terms now.'

Of course, if he is a politician, then it is a thousand times worse.

It is a pity, for it means that the undoubted abilities and energies of Zagreb are being wasted in petty squabbles. It means that the city of Yugoslavia which talks most about democracy is the least democratic in the social sense. In this it is rather like Dublin. In fact, the spiritual attitudes of the two cities are curiously alike.

One of the best roads in Yugoslavia leads from Zagreb to the village of Kumrovec in the Zagorje (the land behind the mountains). This was Tito's birthplace and the house in which he was born has been preserved as a national memorial. Nearby is a small museum of the National Liberation Struggle.

It is a journey well worth-while. The village is an interesting one and the house itself, similar to those around it, has little of the rather stuffy museum atmosphere of most such memorials. It feels as though Tito had only left it recently and that he and his parents might come back to it at any time. Tito is undoubtedly a great leader and little by little a legend has grown up around his name; when he dies, the legendary atmosphere will surely grow stronger. Here, at Kumrovec, one is at the fountainhead and it is pleasant

to find so pure a source. I was lucky enough to visit the little
museum with one of Tito's partisans, who had shared many of his
setbacks and triumphs, so that too came alive.

Zagreb lies in the plain. At Ljubljana you are already in the
foothills of the Alps, and the scenery and way of life are typically
Alpine.

Ljubljana is a pleasant little city, but not especially distinguished.
For the visitor it is mainly a departure point for the lakes and
mountains of Slovenia. Its architecture is mainly Austrian baroque
and its outward appearance Central European. The main feature
of the town is the castle, once rarely shown to visitors, but now the
centre of a pleasant park, with a good restaurant overlooking the
city. The disciplined habits of the Slovenes show themselves in the
neatness and tidiness of their city and their observance, to the
letter, of laws, by-laws and local regulations. This meant that
during the days of political austerity Ljubljana seemed a city laid
under a curse. In other capitals the regulations were more or less
easily circumvented, but not here. It was the more striking in that
pre-war Ljubljana was an exceedingly gay little city.

The Slovene temperament is Slav, but with a great deal of the
order and method of the German. The Slovenes are the best
subordinates of Yugoslavia. They are serious-minded, with a
larger percentage of books published per head than any other
people. They have a great, though recent, literary tradition,
which has produced writers like Prešern and Cankar, and almost
every Slovene knows German, and a large number Italian as well.
With their remaining comrades under Italian rule and those in
America, they number approximately three million. During the
last war the Slovenes came under direct Italian and German rule,
which did not make them love those peoples any the more. Some
of the fiercest partisan fighting was in the Slovene lands.

Disaster hit Skopje, the capital of Macedonia, at 05.17 on July
26th 1963. The city was destroyed by an earthquake. Thanks to
the early hour and the fact that it was the height of the holiday
season when many persons had left the city, which is exceedingly
hot in summer, the death-roll was not as high as it might have been.
Even so, the Macedonian government gives the casualty list as
more than a thousand dead, over four thousand injured and about

80% of the houses in the central part of the city either destroyed or rendered uninhabitable. No-one who knew the city before 1963 would recognize it now.

Earthquake shocks are not uncommon in the Skopje region. Slight tremors are frequent – there was one during my last visit – and the records show more than twenty quakes of Force 6 or more in the first two decades of this century. Twice before the city has been destroyed, in 518 and in 1555. What made the 1963 quake so memorable is that since the liberation of Macedonia Skopje had become a large city with nearly a quarter of a million inhabitants.

Even now there is plenty of devastation to be seen and the Skopje taxi-drivers with a sort of inverted pride go out of their way to show it to visitors. The great buildings by the Stone Bridge have all fallen, most of the mosques are in ruins and many large buildings still standing are death-traps, for the earthquake broke their main support pillars, leaving upper storeys apparently intact. The famous Kuršumli Han (The Leaden Inn), once a caravanserai of the Dubrovnik merchants, has been badly damaged and the Hammam of Daut Pasha (now the city art-gallery), which had survived many previous quakes, was seriously shaken. Only one of the many mosques, the beautiful Muhammed Pasha Mosque, is likely to be repaired and kept as a national monument. The quake twisted the upper part of the minaret, which now hangs over in a seemingly precarious manner. But the restorers say that it can be made safe and they intend to keep it as it is, in memory of that tragic morning.

There is little use now in dwelling on the countless personal tragedies of that July day. A film taken immediately after the quake shows a pathetic queue of people trying to identify the bodies of friends and relatives from little scraps found in the ruins, bits of a dress, a bracelet, etc. Nor are the tragedies over. This year (1965) I found a chambermaid in the main hotel using my telephone. I protested and she explained. Her husband had been killed in the quake and she now went out to work to support her five-year old son. The tremor of the previous night had made the wall of her house collapse and now she was homeless. She was distraught with fear for the boy and was pleading with the authorities for better accommodation.

The destruction of Skopje had one remarkable result which gives one hope for the ultimate brotherhood of man. Within a few hours of the disaster help flowed in by air; first planes with food, medicines and bedding, then construction teams to rebuild the shattered city. Even today, two years later, some of them are still at work. Skopje today is an international city of prefabs from every country in Europe and many in the Americas. There are whole suburbs, including schools, hospitals and technical services, built by those who came to the aid of Skopje: the rest of Yugoslavia, Britain, America, the Soviet Union, France, Italy, Rumania, all the Scandinavian lands and even Mexico, to quote only a few of those equally generous. The result is that Skopje, once a fairly close-packed city, now is twenty-five kilometres square, with consequent problems of communication. A trip through the new suburbs is a revelation in international co-operation. It is a vast blood transfusion of which the world may well be proud, an emotional experience, compound of pity, terror, pride and hope for the future. The visitor must not fail to visit Skopje.

I have already spoken of Titograd, the capital of Montenegro. There remains Sarajevo, the capital of Bosnia and Hercegovina. But of Sarajevo I shall speak in the next chapter.

The village of Gozd Martuljek in Slovenia

CHAPTER XIII

Stepchild of the Centuries: Bosnia

Villages and civilizations – Moslems in Yugoslavia – Virtues and vices of Ottoman rule – Spread of the Bogumils – The sevdalinke, love songs of Bosnia – Bosnian ballads and handicrafts – Travnik, Jajce – A Bogumil shrine – The Bosnian peasant – The Military Frontiers – Valley of the Neretva – Mostar – Sarajevo.

It is not difficult to trace the tradition of any Balkan area by the nature and condition of the villages. In Bosnia they are the most primitive in all Yugoslavia save for the almost-forgotten Homolje district of eastern Serbia, which few people visit. The villages of Macedonia, for instance, still retain traces of the Turkish and Byzantine urban civilizations upon which much of Macedonian culture is founded. There, and in parts of northern Greece and Bulgaria – very occasionally in Bosnia also – one will find remnants of the čifluks. These were manorial settlements, with the huts of the peasants arranged in almost military order around the beg's dwelling, rather like a stricter system of tied cottages. In the free villages the houses of the more well-to-do still have the overhanging balconies and wide first-floor verandas of the typical Anatolian house. The villages of Dalmatia, stone-built and often walled, show the influences of Venice and the West. Often they are very old and incorporate mediaeval and sometimes even Roman remains. The Serbian villages are usually richer, with well-built houses, revealing a developed agricultural life, based on the richness of the soil and the sturdy independence of the peasants. Often, especially in western Serbia, one finds villages still constructed to house the former zadrugas. The name has changed its meaning; in modern Serbian it means simply co-operative, but before and during the times of the insurrection it meant a village founded on close family or tribal organization, with houses extended for the needs of a growing family and with a strict

internal patriarchal rule. Even in the times of Turkish occupation
these villages were semi-independent, with a disciplined family
organization and having little or nothing to do with the Turkish
rulers save the occasional payment of a small tribute. It was
largely from these zadrugas that the leaders of the insurrection
came. The Slovene villages are prosperous and their houses of the
Alpine type not dissimilar to the Swiss chalets. In Croatia and
parts of the plain country one sometimes comes across villages
built at the time of the Military Frontiers, their houses arranged in
neat squares, as fixed and regular as a Roman legionary camp,
showing the military rule and martial discipline of the settlers.
They have their parallel in the Cossack areas of Russia. The
peaceful villages of the plain are built of one-storey houses, surrounded by stalls and outhouses, strung out along the village
street in a sort of ribbon development – an ample proof of the
richness of the soil and the vast amount of space available.

In the Bosnian Marches there are villages of the type of the
Military Frontiers, for the Turks had their own frontiersman
organization, similar to that set up by the Austrians, and also
now and again villages of the čifluk type. But in the forest and
mountain districts, where Islam was never firmly established, one
comes across many tiny villages, often of not more than five or six
houses, scattered over a considerable area, which take one straight
back to the original migrations of the Slavs. Wood is here the main
building material. Being subject to decay and danger of fire, these
villages are seldom old, but the old designs have been repeated
generation after generation. Some of the houses still preserve the
original hearths (there are several technical words for this in
Serbian), with a central stove giving warmth and light to the
inhabitants and with the smoke escaping through a hole in the
roof. Churches are rare and seldom old. The wood construction
made them specially liable to destruction, the Bogumil faith paid
little heed to established centres for prayer and the later Turkish
rule did not encourage their construction. Even today large
church gatherings are always held in the open air. In the more
isolated regions, as also in the Homolje and Sanjak districts, one
may still find small houses rather similar to an Indian wigwam,
and others mounted on crude runners like skis which can be moved

from place to place with the continual migrations of the people. Today these are chiefly used to shelter shepherds on the mountains.

In contrast, there are the neat modern villages, efficient and sometimes very pleasant in appearance, most of which have been built since the last war. For Bosnia was the centre of the partisan resistance, and a very large number of villages were totally destroyed. Those who wish to see what modern Yugoslavia has done in the way of reconstruction are advised to go to Bosnia.

All these are, of course, the Christian villages, mainly Catholic, for the large Orthodox village population of Bosnia was more than decimated after the Ustaša massacres of the last war. The Moslem villages, of which there are many, follow the conventional type, centred around the small square that includes three basic necessities of the village – the mosque, the bakery and the fountain. The houses are of the Turkish type, with inner hidden gardens, wide overhanging balconies and latticed windows, whence the women-folk of the richer inhabitants peered out at the life of the village and perhaps envied their poorer sisters, whom economic necessity granted a greater freedom, drawing water from the fountain which was always the main gathering place and centre of gossip. In some of the older villages one may also find kulas – houses built like a miniature fortress, the lower storeys of loop-holed stone, where the stock could be gathered in times of trouble, while the family lived above in Eastern-style wooden rooms.

The scattered wooden Christian villages among the distant forests and the compact Moslem villages with their fortified kulas represented two sides of a continuing struggle. The first served as hiding-places and refuge for the hajduks, the second as a defence against their raids and as centres whence poteras (punitive expeditions) went forth to destroy them. These hajduks were a typical feature of life under Turkish rule, both in Bosnia and in Serbia itself. Half patriot and half brigand, the hajduks lived by plundering the Turkish population, while at the same time they kept alive the Christian tradition and the feeling for national independence. Sometimes they operated singly, as outlaws, sometimes in bands of about thirty under a recognized leader, somewhat in the Robin Hood tradition. They befriended the peasants of the poorer villages and did much to right their wrongs. In return, they were loved and helped in the long winters when it became impossible to live in the open. There is a special word in Serbian (jatak) for one who shelters a hajduk. The peasants chanted their praises in the heroic ballads, and many of their names have been preserved, as well as many of their deeds, doubtless somewhat exaggerated by the pride and patriotism of the singer. There is a proverb in Serbia: 'The Turks rule the towns, but the hajduks the roads.'

With such a tradition, it is little wonder that in the last war the Yugoslavs proved themselves the world's most dreaded partisan fighters.

It may come as a surprise to many to know that there are well over a million Moslems in Yugoslavia. Most of them are in Bosnia, Hercegovina or the autonomous region of Kosmet (though Macedonia has also many and there are a few in southern Montenegro). Even those who do know this usually call them Turks and assume that they are flotsam left in the Balkans after the Turkish conquest. It is a fairly natural mistake, seeing that Bosnia and Hercegovina were *de facto* Ottoman until 1875 and *de jure* until 1908; and it is further complicated by the fact that they often use the word Turk of themselves, the national and religious ideas having become hopelessly tangled up in their minds. Actually, there have never been many Turks by race in Bosnia and Hercegovina, and not many more in Macedonia, where a few scattered villages of real Turks still remain. Few if any of these Bosnians know Turkish well, and this district is, in fact, celebrated for the purity of its Serbo-Croatian.

The Ottoman power was essentially an empire and not a nation. There was no national feeling, and the difference between conquerors and conquered was one of religion. Many of the greatest men of the Ottoman Empire were Slav or Albanian by origin, and for a long time Serbian was the official language in dealing with foreign ambassadors.

In Serbia the Turkish authorities were the agents of a purely military occupation and lived largely in the few towns, whence they were easily evacuated after the Serbian insurrections. In Macedonia the problem, though more complex, was in essentials similar. But in Bosnia it was quite different. Instead of becoming a Turkish province governed by Turkish officials, Bosnia became a more or less autonomous province governed *de facto* by Moslem descendants of the former Slav nobility, who frequently paid remarkably little attention to the officials sent from Istanbul, who were scarcely permitted within Sarajevo but governed more or less nominally from Travnik or Banja Luka.

The reason for this curious fact must be sought for far back in history and is connected with the somewhat mysterious sect of the Bogumils, whose memorials may still be found in the more distant parts of the country, at Jajce and at Stolac, where there are a large number of magnificent Bogumil tombs with strange carvings and inscriptions, and in the Sarajevo museum.

The sect originated in Bulgaria. We know its earliest precepts largely from its enemies, who describe it as anti-moral and anti-social. The former it can hardly have been, as the extreme ascetics of the sect even eschewed marriage; the second, from a mediaeval viewpoint, it probably was, for it very early developed nationalist tendencies and insisted on the Word of God being preached in the language of the people. This was not to the liking of the Greek priesthood among the Bulgars at that time.

Thence it spread into Macedonia, where it has left many traces on place-names, but was again persecuted by the Nemanjas. In Bosnia, however, it was welcomed and almost became a national church, though its earlier asceticism was much modified and its

Bogumil tombs at Stolac in Hercegovina

antinomian tenets restricted by a rough church organization. The Bogumils might, indeed, be classed as forerunners of the Reformation and, in fact, their influence and teachings strongly affected the Patareni of Milan, the Albigenses of Toulouse and even the Lollards of England.

The Bosnians, then as now, were a political and religious transition between Catholic Croats and Orthodox Serbs who agreed only in regarding their theories of the equal powers of Good and Evil as Manichaean – as indeed they were – and persecuting them. Both also had an eye to their territory. Thus, without Christian support, the Bosnian nobles had no great aversion to being converted to Islam and, incidentally, saving their position and property in the process. A good deal of the so-called conquest of Bosnia was accomplished by the Bosnians themselves; a great part of the long tale of treachery that accompanied it was genuine conversion. The Bosnian feudal lords became Moslem begs and retained their power. The peasantry also followed suit, though to a lesser extent, but still in numbers unheard of in Serbia or Macedonia, and the creation of a Moslem population was in the main a peaceful process.

Many, however, continued their Bogumil rites under the cover of Islam. The last-known Bogumil family, – that of Helež – is supposed to have died out in the village of Dubrovčani as late as 1867.

This mass desertion of their faith by the Bogumil nobles has had a curious result. For the Slav tradition of Bosnia has ever since flowed in two separate and distinct channels; one the Christian peasantry which has kept close to the broad stream of Slav Balkan tradition, enriched by a story-telling facility that is surely Oriental in origin, the other Moslem and aristocratic, a traditional culture of the towns.

It is this second tradition with which the visitor will come most in contact through the antiquarians and artisans of the Sarajevo market, in the form of elaborate brocades, jewelled weapons, intricate silver filigree work and somewhat gaudy Turkish coffee-sets. Its origin is the Istanbul of the sultans, its more recent manifestations only too frequently Birmingham. *Caveat emptor!*

However, some of the old aristocratic tradition has remained, though after the war every effort was made to smother it as a relic of feudalism. This repression, which was both useless and ridiculous, has now, thank goodness, slackened. It would be a very shallow mentality that condemned Greek sculpture on the grounds that Athens was a slave-owning state!

Its most appealing memory are the sevdalinke, the Bosnian love-songs. That is perhaps too simple a method of describing them. The word sevdah is Turkish, and means simply love. But, as transformed by the Bosnians, it has attained a special meaning – something between the helpless love-yearning, bitter and fatalistic, of the Moslem youth, and what the French call *le cafard*. *Od sevdaha goreg jada nema* (There is no more bitter pang than sevdah) runs one of them, unless it be kara-sevdah – black sevdah – when the mind is darkened, life seems useless and the only way out is death.

It is difficult today to hear the sevdalinke sung as they should be sung. For it was essentially an intimate art; they were composed to be sung in the fine old houses of the begs, with their secret gardens, closed courts and quiet fountains. Already before the war they had descended to the kafanas, but they still sounded lovely in the moonlit gardens of Jekovac or Bistrik overlooking Sarajevo. But the curse of the radio and gramophone overwhelemed many of the most charming of these, and the sevdalinke became the property of the gipsies, who sang them noisily and harshly, often with little regard for the music and still less for the words. Now one can hear them only at some Moslem teferič (young people's picnic) to which a visitor may find it hard to get invited.

Even there many of the loveliest old songs have been forgotten, though a few favourites, such as 'When I was walking by Bembasha' or 'How high, how high is the Javorina mountain', seem able to defy the years. Curiously enough, I had the chance of hearing many of the most lovely, long forgotten in their native land, sung in the most perfect surroundings in a great room of an Anatolian house with the windows open on to a bird-haunted garden. It was at Ankara, and the singers were the grandsons and grand-daughters of an old Bosnian beg whose family had fled from Sarajevo after the annexation crisis of 1876. These young people had never been to Bosnia, but they knew the old songs and still spoke the Bosnian dialect among themselves. It was strangely parallel to Cecil Sharp's discovery of old English folk-songs in the Appalachian Mountains.

The Christian peasant tradition is best shown in costumes, folk-music and handicrafts. But the Moslem peasant tradition has developed a very interesting series of national ballads. Basically similar to those of the Christian Serbs and Macedonians, heroes and villains have, of course, changed places, and it is the Moslem who is battling for the preservation and extension of his faith. Marko Kraljević and the Nemanjas are replaced by Kapedan Pasha or Kulin Ban. Amongst them, too, one will find poems that have completely by-passed the national and historical tradition of the Christian ballads and stem from still older Oriental sources. Probably they have been influenced by the sevdalinke, though there is some doubt which is the older. The story of Omer and Merima, for example, goes back at least to the Arabian Nights, if not before. These two star-crossed lovers die without fulfilment, and from their graves grow two rose-trees that intertwine and become a single stem.

It is curious that neither among the Christian nor the Moslem peasants is there any tradition of the older Bosnian kingdom before the Turkish conquest. They will tell you gladly of Marko Kraljević, Stefan Lazarević or Kulin Ban, but they know absolutely nothing of Tvrtko, Hrvoje Vukčić or Stjepan Tomašević, who were equally great figures in their day.

The Bosnian trains are slow and stertorous. Most visitors avoid them and use the tourist bus services, which pass through the more interesting towns: Banja Luka, Travnik, Jajce, Sarajevo and Mostar. But those with more time at their disposal will find it well worth visiting the forest country of north-west Bosnia. Until the discovery, or rather the exploitation – for the deposits were known before Roman times – of iron ore in the water-shed of the Bosna, timber was the wealth of Bosnia. It is still an important industry.

The area is difficult of access, the dense forests covering vast mountain ranges, of which one gets an excellent view from the plane between Belgrade and Split. Indeed, so isolated are many of the villages that the peasants are far more familiar with the planes that pass overhead than with trains or motor-cars, neither of which have they had any occasion to see save in their period of military service. It was probably just because of this isolation that this north-west corner of Bosnia was the first area to be liberated by the partisan armies and that the first assembly of the new government was held at Jajce. Here it is that one will hear the most stirring stories of the partisan wars, from the days when the partisans were still guerrillas and before the formation of the proletarian brigades. It was in the heart of this country, at Drvar, that a daring German parachute raid nearly captured the whole of the General Staff, including Tito himself. Had it succeeded, the course of the partisan wars might have been different, for this previously unknown leader proved himself a most excellent soldier and a personal inspiration to his men, even to those who did not always agree with his political ideas.

When I myself last visited the forest country, it was from the south, from Sarajevo by way of Travnik to Jajce, where I was allowed to make use of the forest railway.

The rail journey was slow, hot and wearisome. But the first sight of Travnik is worth much weariness. One comes upon it suddenly around a bed of the Lašva valley in which it is built. It was for many years the seat of the Bosnian viziers, who made it beautiful and, though it has been badly damaged by wars and by a disastrous fire, it is still beautiful. A rapid glance reveals houses of the finest period of Bosnian Moslem architecture, luxuriant gardens filled with fruit trees, and a tremendous fortress built by the Bosnian kings.

Jajce is one of the most strikingly beautiful cities of Yugoslavia. But I should not like to live with that beauty always before my eyes. The canvas is over-charged. There is no feeling of rest. It would be like living in a small room with a Rubens.

It is built on a conical hill, with the castle of Hrvoje Vukčić on the summit. Just outside the walls the picturesque Bosnian houses clamber up the slopes, their dark, tent-like shapes broken by the lovely Venetian campanile of the Church of St Luke, a few minarets, and the squat form of the Bear Tower. Around the hills flows the river Pliva in a series of picturesque cascades which culminate in a terrific waterfall where the Pliva descends into the narrow canyon of the Vrbas. It is astounding, but disturbing.

Incidentally, it must be one of the most photographed places in the world.

Though the greatness of Jajce was limited to a bare hundred years, it has in that time managed to collect around it a cloud of legend. For it was the last stronghold of the Bosnian kingdom, the scene of the last desperate stand of the South Slavs to maintain an independent state before the long centuries of Ottoman rule. The site was occupied in Neolithic and Roman times, but does not seem to have had any special significance before the Bosnian Hrvoje Vukčić built the fortress here (1391–1404). This was the same Hrvoje who was lord of Split, and whom the canons of that city cursed as Pharaoh. It seems that he was a Bogumil, or at

*The falls
of the Pliva
river at Jajce
in Bosnia*

least tolerated that creed, and his life and that of his successors was taken up in a continual struggle against the Hungarians, which weakened their resistance to the victorious Turks.

Here, too, was executed the last king of Bosnia, Stjepan Tomašević, in 1463. He was a weak-kneed sort of character, but his death has lent him a sort of halo. Legend has it that he was executed by the Turkish leader in person, who excused the treachery by which he succeeded in capturing him with the words: 'None but a fool gets bitten twice by a snake from the same hole.'

The Bosnian kingdom may seem of little importance to us now. But it bulked large in its day. Despite its heresy, the Doge of Venice wrote to Pope Pius II: 'Before our eyes, the richest kingdom in the world is burning', while Mathias Corvinus, who contributed very greatly to its downfall, referred to it as 'the harbour of Christianity'. The Turks, too, realized the value of their conquest. After the peace of Karlovci they refused to exchange the war-devastated Bosnian March for rich lands in Wallachia. 'These towns', they said, 'are the gateway to Constantinople.' Certainly they were the gateway to Sarajevo.

In the fortress of Jajce, Hrvoje Vukčić built himself a catacomb. Whether it was intended as a church or as a tomb is uncertain. What on earth induced him to hew it out of the solid rock of the citadel, when he had above ground one of the most splendid sites in Europe, is almost beyond comprehension. But there it is. One descends into a chapel of considerable size and then lower still into a vault with empty recesses and a large altar. Apparently he was challenged by death before he had finished his preparations for meeting it. At any rate, the work is unfinished and the walls undecorated save for the Vukčić coat-of-arms near the door and some Bogumil symbols over the main altar. But it is awesome in its dank solidity, and must have been even more so before the municipality put in a few feeble electric bulbs. It is also very cold. After the heat of the summer day outside, the vault is like a refrigerator.

It is curious why a man like Vukčić should have chosen this chilly cavern for his family tomb. Most men of his power and period would have demanded display; but here it is even far from easy to find the entrance. The Bogumils were a curious sect.

Perhaps there was in his mind some analogy with the early days of the persecuted Christians.

As far as Jajce is concerned, it has excellent roads and a good motor-bus service, which continues along the gorge of the Vrbas as far as Banja Luka, where the normal railway system again commences (incidentally, the line from Banja Luka to Zagreb was the first line ever built in the Ottoman Empire). But the forest country is ill served by communications and is the most primitive of all the districts of Yugoslavia, except the Homolje district of eastern Serbia.

This is not entirely the fault of the Yugoslavs. Much money is needed to develop a devastated district, and the Bosnian March may truly be so described. It was for centuries the battlefield of the fierce soldiers of the Croatian Military Frontiers and of the Martolossi, which were the Ottoman equivalent. Life and property were insecure and the people brutish and depraved. During the last war it was again devastated, perhaps more terribly and thoroughly than in the days of the Military Frontiers.

I have, on the whole, so far drawn a fairly favourable picture of Ottoman rule. In fact it was for centuries very much better than the Yugoslav historians like to describe it. Even now there are peasants of the older generation who regret its swift, if unequal justice and its clearly defined code of privileges and duties. But when the central authority weakened, whether at Istanbul or Sarajevo, the local begs and spahis got out of hand and ruled with the worst excesses of the feudal system. Each section of the Empire did much as it pleased, and although there were a few wise and tolerant men, like Mustafa Pasha, 'the Mother of the Serbs', the Ottoman pashas and valis for the most part became drunk with power and misused it horribly. Those appointed by Stamboul only thought to get rich quickly before they were re-placed by a richer or more cunning intriguer, while those who had become more or less independent only thought to consolidate their position. The pashas of Yanina, Skadar or Vidin ruled like independent princes; the begs of Sarajevo changed viziers almost at their will, while the murder of Mustafa Pasha by the Belgrade janissaries led to a period of oppression that was the cause of the insurrection of Karageorge and the eventual liberation of the

Serbian people. In Bosnia and Hercegovina the extortions of the tax-gatherers led to a series of revolts, culminating in the Neresinje insurrection of 1875, the direct cause of the Austrian occupation.

It is mainly from this period that one reads of the Turkish atrocities that so inflamed the liberal conscience of Europe. Most of them were too ghastly for Victorian stomachs, and even now it is not pleasant to describe them in detail. Impalement was a common punishment. The living victim was spitted on a sharp stake, which entered the body at the crotch of the legs and emerged about the back of the neck. In this condition, if tough – and the Serbs and Bosnians are tough – he might linger on for several days. It is described with gruesome detail in Ivo Andrić's magnificent chronicle *The Bridge on the Drina*.

There is little wonder, then, that the Bosnian peasant became suspicious and brutish, and that some echoes of those methods have been carried on to the present day in times of crisis. The Turks used to say: '*Krk bosnak bir adam*' – Forty Bosnians, one man – but they were themselves largely responsible. It is a great tribute to the character of the Bosnian peasant today that he is, for the most part, hospitable and good-humoured towards strangers, though still slower-witted than his Serb or Croat kinsmen. I have heard tales of those times from men whose grandfathers and grandmothers had to undergo such tortures. The ingenious gentlemen who write such literature as *The Pleasures of the Torture Chamber* would do well to investigate the past of Bosnia. It is also little wonder that the Bosnian regiments were the most reckless and ferocious of the former Austro-Hungarian army and were the terror of the Italians on the Piave front in the First World War. Their warlike abilities have in no way degenerated since.

To the average visitor Bosnia and Hercegovina means Sarajevo and Mostar; and the chances are that he will approach them either from Split or from Dubrovnik along the valley of the Neretva.

The railway from Dubrovnik is not a good line; but it is a wonder that there is a line there at all. It is narrow-gauge, slow, and intolerably stuffy, though there is now an excellent diesel train in the tourist season. It crawls slowly upwards in intricate serpentines over the mountains behind the Dubrovačka Rijeka.

By leaning out of the window one may see the outflow of the Ombla, which breaks full fledged from the rock after a subterranean course of many miles, and within a few yards of it large ships lying at anchor. First on one side, then on the other, one looks down at the most lovely panorama of shining blue sea, graceful and solemn cypresses, and the old stone-built summer palaces of the former Dubrovnik patricians.

Then a patch of bare stone, and then the last view of the Adriatic, the bay of Dubrovnik with Cavtat in the distance and a tiny white dot that is the Meštrović mausoleum. Then naked karst and the sun-scorched station of Uskoplje.

But in July the karst is not quite so forbidding. The summer heats have not yet scorched its shallow-rooted grasses. The pomegranates are just beginning to turn from flame-coloured blossom into bulbous fruit. Tall yellow flowers stand defiantly in the chinks of the stones. In the tiny, cup-like vrtače of red earth, which alone are cultivable, there are still tufts of green maize or, more rarely, yellow corn. It is already too high and exposed for olives, but there are still figs and the first whiteish flowers of the autumn pumpkins. It is not so grim and impressive as in winter, but it is more friendly.

Then we creep down once more to the Popovo polje, whose exact nature always worries the inquisitive tourist. In spring it is a vast shallow lake, with little red-roofed villages along its stony banks. But in early summer the waters sink away into underground ghylls, or ponors, leaving a shallow but rich deposit of reddish earth, which is extraordinarily fertile. Sometimes the peasants get two, or even three, crops from it before the waters rise again to replenish it. So waterless is it in high summer that every village has its cistern to preserve drinking-water, for the river is not a mere trickle; it disappears altogether. Now, in July, it is a field of young corn and broad-leafed tobacco plants. For the Hercegovinian tobacco is excellent, and many connoisseurs prefer its broad leaves to the smaller, more aromatic leaves of the Macedonian tobacco.

Tobacco is one of the most important Yugoslav products, and the cigarette tobacco is excellent. It is of the Oriental type, usually known as Turkish. Much of the best Turkish tobacco comes from the valleys of the Struma and Strumica in Bulgaria and Yugoslavia, while the favourite flavouring tobacco comes from Kavalla in northern Greece.

But to return to our journey. At Gabela we enter the valley of the Neretva. It is not far from Metković, yet how different a landscape! For the river is no longer olive and dirtied, but flows with a clear pure green which becomes more and more intense as one advances up the valley, until at Mostar it is like emerald watered silk. The trees are heavy with fruit: figs and golden apricots.

Just beyond Čapljina, on the far side of the river, is one of the most lovely cities of Hercegovina – Počitelj. Unfortunately a thick clump of trees screens most of the view from the train, so that the passer-by has only a momentary glimpse. The man with a car is luckier: he can stop and investigate.

He can also take his car to storied Stolac, seat of the terrible Smail Aga Čengić, where there is a strange Bogumil cemetery with huge sarcophagus-like tombs with strange carvings and inscriptions.

At Počitelj the regular rectangle of the walls, climbing up the steep river-bank, gives one the impression that the whole city has been tipped forward by a kindly djinn in order that one may 'see the works'. In the mathematical centre of the rectangle is a fine mosque, with the usual square sahat-kula (clock-tower) behind. Počitelj is first mentioned in 1448, but is probably older, for the Hungarian king-errant Mathias Corvinus garrisoned it in 1465 against the Turks, who none the less took it under Haza Beg in 1471. Under them it became a small but strong fortress, and after the destruction of Gabela by the Venetians in 1715, the most important in the lower Neretva valley. The mosque was built in 1562 by a certain Hadži Alija, but was later repaired by one of the famous sons of Počitelj, Šišman Ibrahim Pasha, who became vali of Egypt. His first name has a curiously Bogumil ring about it.

The whole Neretva gorge is very beautiful and the train follows the river faithfully along a series of fertile poljes; first that of Gabela and then, after an interval of sterile stone, that of Mostar. Here the river Buna joins the Neretva in a series of cascades. One can just see the deserted mosque and the old coffee-houses near

The town of Počitelj on the Neretva river

the source of that river which, like the Ombla, issues in full stream from the mountain-side. The coolness and the excellent trout of this charming spot made it a favourite summer resort of the Moslem begs.

A minor digression; the wonderful old 'Roman bridge' across the Neretva at Mostar is, of course, not Roman, but Turkish. The name derives from the fact that it was built by Dalmatian masons who were known to the local inhabitants as 'Latini'.

At each station most of the passengers rushed out to the drinking-water pumps with cups, bottles and utensils of every description. The heat was intense; water spilled on the track literally dried before one's eyes. At first I had laughed at the bottle maniacs. But as early as Gabela I had acquired a bottle of my own, and was soon leading the gang.

The Mostar polje is literally the meeting of East and West. The houses of Mostar itself are still stone-built and the streets paved in the Mediterranean manner. But the gardens and the mosques and the little familiar coffee-houses are definitely Bosnian. Nature, too, has chosen Mostar as a frontier. Here are the last figs and apricots and the first walnuts and chestnuts. Hercegovina is mostly karst, Bosnia mostly forest, and the Ivan Planina which divides the two also divides the watersheds of the Adriatic and the Black Sea.

It is a curious feeling to stand on the banks of some river, not fifty miles from the Adriatic, such as the Sana or the Kupa, and to think that the stream at one's feet eventually discharges into the Black Sea. The Black Sea watershed is enormous; that of the Adriatic short and precipitous.

Nearly at the top of the divide, at Jablanica, a new hydro-electric plant and dam has created a great lake several kilometres long, with bathing beaches and water sports. It is a curious sight, high up in the Bosnian mountains, whose passes, almost inaccessible in winter, were the scene of some of the toughest battles of the partisan wars.

Then the train crawls over the Ivan Planina, where the peasants offer to the tired and dirty passengers little baskets of wood strawberries or bunches of wild asparagus, and pants its way thankfully downhill towards Sarajevo.

As with so many of the Yugoslav towns, it would require a

volume to give an indication of the whole history of Sarajevo. The site is very ancient, as is shown by the existence of a rich Neolithic settlement in the vicinity. Under the Bosnian kings, however, it was a fortress, Vrh Bosna, and little more. Its real development was after the Turkish conquest, and the tradition of the city is largely Moslem.

The former Sarajevo market, the Baš Čaršija, was much damaged during the war. To the destruction wrought by air-raids was added the more widespread destruction of fire, for the tiny oriental shops were mostly of wood. But enough remains to give an exotic character to the centre of Sarajevo. The wide streets and new suburbs are mainly industrial. Sarajevo, like Skopje, has resolutely turned its back on the past, which is gradually being relegated to museums, and is moving with giant, if uncertain, strides into the future. But the lovely walk along the Miljacka river, where in the evenings the air is heavy with the scent of the lindens, is as beautiful as ever.

Many of the most interesting places in the city are on the Miljacka. One is the Bendbaša café. The word Bendbaša means 'the last weir' and it was there that the timber merchants used to sit and wait for their logs which were rafted down the Miljacka. Each recognized his own goods by his brand and carried on business in comfort, drinking coffee on the balconies overlooking the river. But now the Miljacka has been canalized and there are no more rafts.

Another is the Princip Bridge, with a plaque commemorating the assassination there of the Austrian Archduke Franz Ferdinand that led to the outbreak of the First World War. The events of that tragic day – incidentally another anniversary of the fateful Vidovdan – are well known and need no recapitulation. Historians still argue about the precise degree of complicity of the Serbian government, which was probably nil, though some Serb secret societies undoubtedly knew a great deal about it, as also about the precise degree of provocation on the part of the Austro-Hungarian government, which was considerable. The point to be remembered, however, is that to the Yugoslavs Princip was a patriot. Whatever one's views about the nature of his patriotism, it is undoubtedly true that the consequences of his action led to the downfall of the

Hapsburg Empire and, eventually, to the liberation and union of the Yugoslavs.

On the hillside above Bendbaša is the fortress. It is comparatively recent in date, for in its great days Sarajevo was an open town far from the frontier. The fortress quarter housed the most distinguished families, and still possesses the most beautiful Moslem homes, with wide latticed čardak-balconies and gardens and beautifully wrought iron door-handles. It was a purely residential quarter, and there were no shops save the necessary bakers; for Moslem families mix their bread and cakes at home and then send them to the public baker. The main street used to have a mountain stream running down the centre, driving twelve water-mills.

On the other side of the Miljacka is the suburb of Bistrik, where I found refuge in the house of a carpenter in the late stages of the 1941 bombing. Its steep, winding streets are delightful and it is full of strange holes and corners. The paved road leading there is the commencement of the Stambul Djol, the old military road to Constantinople, along which the Tatars carried messages to the Sultan in swift-footed relays. Post couriers were known as Tatars long after the last of that race had disappeared from Bosnia.

One of the most surprising features about Sarajevo – as, for that matter, about most large Moslem towns – is the graveyards. You find them in the most unlikely places. There are graves in the public park, beside the main cinema and in the centre of one of the principle streets. Often they are very small, with perhaps five or six turbaned headstones. Usually the graves are grass-grown and anonymous, with perhaps a sword, to show the inmate was a janissary, or a text from the Koran. One here in Bistrik is more than usually desolate and the memorials mostly blocks of uncarved stone. It was the strangers' graveyard. When a foreigner died in Sarajevo, it was here that he was buried, so that his friends, if they came, would know where to find his grave.

Incidentally, the desolate and anonymous nature of most Moslem graveyards has become a proverb among the Yugoslav Christians. If you wish to describe something as more than usually dreary and depressing you compare it with a 'tursko groblje'.

Perhaps the finest view over Sarajevo, the most lovely city of the Balkans, is from the top of Hosein Breg. One looks down over the many mosques, some of them beautiful works of architecture, like the Careva or the Begova or those of Gazi Ali-Pasha or Cekrekčija Muslihuddin; others simple houses with stumpy wooden minarets. Before the sack and burning of Sarajevo by Prince Eugene of Savoy in 1697 there were still more. By great good chance, however, the best of them, being made of stone, survived.

Sarajevo was built on the spot where the gorge of the Miljacka begins to widen into a valley. But the city soon outgrew its limits and sprawled contentedly on the steep mountain slopes on either side. The city lies spread out before one as on a map. In the dusk, the setting sun picks out the minarets, the white headstones of the cemeteries and the clumps of tall poplars, turning them to shining silver and dark bronze. In the little wooden kiosks of the hillside cafés there is usually a pleasant breeze from the mountains.

Near the Town Hall, on the far side of the Miljacka, is the station for the cable railway which runs to the summit of Trebević (about 5,000 feet), and beyond that again the gaunt Jahorina and Romanija mountains, once the hideouts of the hajduks and now fashionable ski-slopes in winter. As the car sails upward one catches fascinating glimpses of the closed gardens of the little oriental houses, and on the summit there is a café terrace where one can sit peaceably sipping coffee in the sunset light looking down over Sarajevo.

CHAPTER XIV

The Way Home: Slovenia

The Slovene language – Yugoslav dialects – A historical enigma – Moun-taineering – Maribor Castle – Glass painting and bee-hive boards – Slovene wines – A baroque church – Bled and Bohinj, contrasts in beauty – Serenity and loneliness – Triglav, Home of the Gods – Slovenj-gradec.

Slovenia is quite distinct from the rest of Yugoslavia. Landscape, temperament, history, tradition and language – all are different. The common bond is race.

The landscape is Alpine. Slovenia is the eastern continuation of the Alpine system of Switzerland and the Tyrol. At first glance one might be in either of those two countries. Only a closer inspection reveals that all the older churches, whose towers are so typical of the countryside, are or have been fortified against Turkish raids; and one also notices that all the signs are in a Slav language. But the high, snow-covered peaks, the wooden, chalet-like houses, the flower-spattered upland pastures, the little saw-mills and the rich flocks are familiar. Only here the rivers run to the east, uniting at last to form the mighty Sava, the main road to Belgrade and the East.

The Slovene language is comprehensible to the Serb or Croat, but has marked differences. It is far more archaic and complicated and, incidentally, far more difficult to learn. After Serbian, it sounds curiously explosive, but the great Slovene poets have turned it to melodious and pleasing rhythms. As in all mountain districts, there are very many sub-dialects, of which the literary language is a more or less artificial adaptation.

It is worth mentioning here that all the spoken variants of the Yugoslav language merge into one another as one travels from west to east. Slovene is considered a separate language rather than a dialect, largely because of the crystallization of its literary forms, which have preserved many features of the old Slav tongue that have been toned down by use, or omitted altogether, in the revision of the Serbian and Croatian variants as recreated in the literary language based on the reforms of Vuk Stefan Karadžić. But the gradations of the spoken language are far more gradual. The town speech of Zagreb approximates much more closely to Slovene than the language of books or newspapers. One of the greatest works of the Croat poet, Miroslav Krleža, the 'Balade Petrice Kerempuha', which was written in the Zagreb kaj-dialect of the eighteenth century, seems today almost as much Slovene as Croatian. As one travels east, one comes to the areas of the što-dialect. The language becomes harder and more virile; also there is a larger percentage of Turkish loan-words, and fewer German ones, in everyday speech. Still farther east, and the characteristic case-endings of Serbian tend to drop away – the people of Niš are proverbial for their carelessness in this matter – while Macedonian, recently advanced to the dignity of a language, even begins to use the suffixed article which is a feature of Bulgarian and sometimes makes that language sound like the rattle of a machine-gun. In fact, education, while increasing literacy, has multiplied linguistic barriers.

But to return to the Slovenes.

Slovene history is a puzzle to the Englishman, who finds it hard to understand a struggle for liberty lasting over a thousand years in which scarcely a single incident of historical importance occurs. In fact, the most wonderful thing about the Slovenes is that they exist at all as a nation, after so many centuries of foreign rule.

The Slovenes settled in their present homes in the early sixth century, replacing the Celto-Roman inhabitants of earlier times, partly as independent tribes under their own princes, partly as tributaries of the Avars. After the Avars had been annihilated by the Franks, Slovenia became a frontier march of the Empire under Charlemagne. A frontier march it remained throughout most of its history, under various Markgraves, now defending the Empire against the Hungarians, now against other Slavs, later against the Turks. Throughout the whole of feudal times it made only three appearances on the stage of history: a brief period of glory under the powerful counts of Celje, a brilliant revival of national feeling and language during the Reformation under Primož Trubar, and a participation in the peasant revolts. Later, under the Dual Monarchy, the Slovenes came directly under Austrian rule and their powerful nobles were merely a German ruling caste. During this time the few towns were almost completely germanized. Slovene was scarcely spoken and Austrian art and architecture triumphed everywhere. Its influence is still very marked today. But, as with all Slav races, the real strength of the people lay in the peasants, who remained uncompromisingly Slav and developed in their own way in their distant mountain valleys. Goldsmith's 'rude Carinthian boor' probably thought he was shutting the door on a German.

The formation of the Illyrian province of Napoleon re-awoke dormant national feeling. Ljubljana became the administrative centre and Slovene was admitted to equality with French and German. This was the first period of revived Slovene literature, and the Slovene poets celebrated Napoleon as a deliverer.

When the Slovenes fell once more under Austrian rule, national feeling was already awake and active. The Slovene people produced great writers and philologists who stressed the Slav origin of their people. It was Kopitar who encouraged and assisted Vuk Stefan Karadžić, the founder of the modern Serbo-Croat language and literature. The Slovene Church, too, took a hand, helping the people and encouraging the feeling of nationality. Bishop Slomšek, one of the stoutest nationalists, is almost a saint to the Slovenes.

In 1870 the Croats and Slovenes made a common statement of their Yugoslav aims. Attempts to germanize the country became less and less successful. After the First World War, under their leader Antun Korošec, they voted for union with the Serbs and Croats.

This long struggle was none the less bitter even though without major incident. It has left the Slovene with a sincere admiration for the German, but with an equally sincere distrust of his methods and intentions. The same applies even more, since the last war, to the Italian. Their culture has always been overshadowed by Germany, but their sympathies, when not purely clerical – for they are devoted, almost bigoted, Catholics – turn towards France and

England, who have, and can have, no territorial ambitions at their expense.

The experiences of the Slovenes during the war were not calculated to make them feel any kindlier to their powerful neighbours. While Croatia was granted at least a puppet autonomy, Slovenia was ignominiously degraded to a province; the greater part was annexed by Italy and the rest by the Third Reich. But two decades of freedom had given self-confidence to the Slovenes. Instead of, as in the past, meekly submitting to their new masters, a vigorous resistance movement sprang up and soon established contact with the main resistance group of Marshal Tito.

The Slovenes have not the warrior traditions of the Serbs, or even the Croats whose military reputation was considerable in the later Middle Ages, though largely in the service of foreign overlords. But they are extremely intelligent and well organized, and these qualities are of almost more value than brute courage in the complexities of modern war. Also, their position as a province had one great advantage over that of the Serbs and Croats, albeit a negative one. They had no quisling government, and had a long and intimate acquaintance with the vices and virtues of their wartime masters. Also of their languages; almost every educated Slovene speaks German almost as well as his native language and very many, especially those from Istria and the Julian March, know Italian.

Furthermore, they are great sportsmen and active mountaineers who know every crag and corner of their exceedingly mountainous land. Every young Slovene is an expert skier, as one can see from the crowded excursion trains that leave Ljubljana or Maribor for the mountain resorts every week-end or holiday. Save for the Scandinavians, who originated the word and popularized the pastime, the Slovenes are the only people with words of their own for skis and ski-ing, which has been known and practised in Slovenia for centuries. A Slovene writer and historian, Valvasor, mentions them in the seventeenth century, and describes the peasants on the plateau of Bloka, near Ljubljana, as walking on the snow with the aid of planks and descending the snow-slopes with the speed of devils.

Once across the borders of the Federal Republic of Slovenia, the river Sava changes character. From a broad and dignified water-way, it becomes a fast-rushing mountain river. You can find trout here; in the muddy waters of the lower reaches they would stifle.

At the junction of Zidani Most the train turns into the valley of the Savinja, past Celje, for Maribor.

When I was first at Maribor, the great hall of the castle was a cinema. Now, thanks to the efforts of the local lovers of art, the castle has been purged of its intruders, various later accretions have been removed and the whole building restored to something like its previous beauty. In particular the cloister-like galleries have been cleared. They were probably the work of Domenico de Lalio, who restored the castle in 1544, after it had been badly damaged in a Turkish raid. Those galleries are beautiful, but look a little strange at Maribor. They are more reminiscent of the south than of the home of winter sports.

The castle is a mixture of styles, Gothic, Renaissance and baroque, but age has weathered them into a unity. Now that the rubbish of the last 150 years is cleared away, the castle again represents the Mark-burg, as it had done for centuries.

Generally speaking, the baroque had spread unchecked over Slovenia. I myself do not like its tawdry tinsel, despite one or two fine examples that I have to admire in spite of myself. But sometimes the older and more native Gothic can still be found, and when it is found it is beautiful. Modern Slovene taste inclines among the intellectuals to modernism and among the peasants to the traditional and by now familiar baroque. An example of this at its best – or worst, according to taste – is the column erected in the main square in 1681 to commemorate the cessation of the terrible plague that followed the Thirty Years War. The statue was added later, in 1743.

In the Maribor museum are some lovely wood-carvings of the Gothic period and a glass-painting apparently by Dürer.

It is not, however, in the naïve style of the peasant glass-painting, which is unfortunately dying out. These pictures, actually on glass, painted by a lasting process, which has survived the centuries, are not great works of art, but they are extremely charming, by reason of their gay colours and deep religious sense.

They are dying out for a very practical reason: they were originally so painted that the holy figures might survive the smoky winters in the little Alpine huts. In other words, that the Holy Saints might be periodically washed. Now that housing has improved, their reason for existence has gone.

Another art, which I believe to be peculiar to Slovenia, is the beautiful painting of the beehive boards, decorated with scriptural scenes and figures of saints or, more rarely, secular heroes. A group of twenty or thirty of these box-like hives, each with its gaily painted panel, is a lovely sight which may still be seen, although the modern Slovene peasant mostly uses plain washes of colour. The best specimens are now in museums.

Yet another thing typical of Slovenia is the klapotec, or wind-rattle, used to scare birds from the vineyards. Slovene poets have used it as the symbol of their country.

Slovene wines are well known in England. They have the advantage over the Serbian and Dalmatian wines, which I myself prefer for flavour, in that they are more stable, travel better and are more standardized. The best known are the wines of Ljutomer, Gorica and Radgona, which are sold under these regional names with the addition of the name of the type of grape from which they are made: Riesling (sec), Sylvaner (demi-sec), Sauvignon (demi-sec and also very dry) and Traminer (demi-sec). There is also a white sparkling wine, which comes from the Ljutomer vineyards and was sold in Yugoslavia before the war as Slovene (in very small letters) Champagne. It is now sold, somewhat inappropriately, as Duc de Slovenie. I do not like it very much, but that is a personal taste, as I do not like sparkling wines in general.

The standard vin du pays in Slovenia is a vin rosé, very slightly acid, known as cviček. Probably because it is the commonest wine in the taverns, a good many atrocities are committed in its name. But its export quality is excellent and its flavour blends very happily with the Kranj sausages, a local delicacy better known in this country under their German name of krainerwurst.

Two of the most famous vineyard villages of this part of Slovenia are called Jerusalem and Bethlehem. The story goes, and it is not unlikely, that part of a crusading army passing through Slovenia on its way to the Holy Land were so taken with the country-side that they decided to forego their long journey and find here their Promised Land. They did so, and named their villages accordingly.

The Slovenes are wine- and beer-drinkers. The strong spirits of Serbia, Bosnia and Croatia are not distilled here, nor are they drunk to the same extent. But there are wide hop-fields and very extensive vineyards.

It may be that the Alpine landscape, with its lonely valleys and snow-capped mountains, exercises a peculiar spell. I know that it is true of myself and I have noticed it often enough in others. When I am in Slovenia I have not the same interest in art, in history, in people, as I have in the other districts of Yugoslavia, and I have many friends in England who would not dream of going to France, Italy or Spain without having at least a superficial background, a literary frame in which to place their impressions, but who return from Switzerland or the Tyrol without the smallest idea of those countries. I could not spend a day in the comparatively uninterest-ing Voivodina without wanting to know more about it, whereas I have spent months in Slovenia and come back with no more than a general impression of having spent a very pleasant holiday. One spends all day in the open air, making endless excursions. Nature has so far outstripped man in her creations that the towns and villages of Slovenia seem only a background to her master-pieces; whereas the mountains and ravines of Macedonia, of Dalmatia or of Montenegro seem only the background to the human dramas that have been played out there amongst them. It is the same with the literature of the Alpine lands. The interest is in the landscape; the characters are only too often bloodless puppets.

The most popular resort in Slovenia is Bled. For one thing, it has plenty of good hotels; for another, it was the summer capital where ruler and ministers retired when the summer heats of Bel-grade became violent and oppressive. The custom was started by King Alexander, who had a castle on a bluff by the lakeshore. Marshal Tito continued it after the war, though now he usually spends more time on the island of Brioni, off the Istrian coast. Consequently Bled has become a social centre of importance whose visiting list of distinguished guests from abroad becomes yearly longer.

I have spent several holidays at Bled, both in and out of season. The impression that remains is that of a lovely lake among mountains, surrounded by luxurious hotels, with little gondolas gliding over smooth water to and from the island church in the centre of the lake. One month spent in Bled in winter before the snow was deep enough for ski-ing recalls to me the picture of dark reeds, lit by gleams of light from the terrace of the Hotel Toplica, receding into soft, velvety darkness, and of being awakened in the morning by the groaning and cracking of the ice forming on the lake, which echoed among the mountains like the grumbling of giants or the distant artillery of some celestial war. Yes, and I must add the picture of the peasant women on home-made skis and skates gliding over the ice to the church in the centre of the lake.

I remember also unforgettable days on the Lake of Bohinj, where the mountains rise so high that the waters in the early morning and at twilight seem almost black. At the lower end of the lake is the lovely little Gothic church of St Janež.

For myself, I prefer Bohinj to Bled. Bohinj is wilder and more awesome; Bled calm and lovely, but more open and familiar. One might call Bled a beautiful and placid blonde, Bohinj a tempestuous and incalculable brunette.

I remember, too, the serenity and loneliness of the Logar valley, and have spent happy months in the valley that leads from Jesenice on the Austrian frontier to Rateče. For sheer beauty and comfort, it is perhaps the best place for a summer or winter holiday in Yugoslavia. The mountains here are sheer and precipitous, more imposing than the rounded summits of the Pohorje near Maribor. Mountaineers tell me that they are better, and ski-ers that they are not so good. I cannot judge, as I am only a moderate mountaineer and have never mastered skis. But the villages are lovely and the mountains superb. There is nothing so restful as to lie in some flower-strewn meadow high up on the slopes after a sharp climb and look down at the peaceful valley below or up at the snow-peaks above. There one can achieve the impossible – namely, to do absolutely nothing save lie still without thoughts and without desires, and let the changing patterns of the clouds or the changing colours of the mountains pass before one's eyes in a passionless content. I have stayed in Kranjska Gora for more than a month – one of the most perfect holidays of my life. But I never even went inside the church and could not say now what was its period. Sir Humphry Davy, the great scientist, lived for years in this valley, in the little village of Podkoren, and thought it the most beautiful spot in the world. His house is marked with a tablet. A little farther on at Rateče Planica there is the mammoth ski-jump where world records are made. It was at Planica that a peasant woman once offered me a baby deer as a pet. It was a charming little animal, curled up contentedly in a wicker basket, and quite tame; but I remembered my crowded flat in Belgrade and regretfully declined it.

Slovenia is a comfortable land to wander in. There are excellent maps of all the mountains which mark the main paths. (By the way, the curious-looking inscription 'Peš pot' merely means footpath.) The Slovenes have also built excellent and exceedingly comfortable mountain hostels in the most unlikely places to aid serious mountaineers. But they do very well for the dilettante, too. They have good food and always excellent company; usually in the evenings they are full of mountaineers making ready for a stiff climb early next morning. One or other of them always has a harmonica, and everybody sings. They even yodel. The Slovene songs, too, are typically Alpine. But the Slav tongue gives them a piquancy, and though not musically very interesting they are exceedingly gay and tuneful. I remember one of these hostels in particular, built in a wide meadow with a tiny mountain stream running through it, directly under the stupendous north wall of the Triglav.

Triglav, meaning the three-headed, is the highest peak in Yugoslavia and has almost a religious significance for the Slovenes. It was the Olympus of the Slav gods, and many legends are associated with it, particularly the lovely story of the Zlatorog, the golden-antlered stag.

It was partly the name that took me to Slovenjgradec. It means 'the Slovene citadel', and the adjective served to differentiate it from the Bavarian Graz (or Gradec) that is now simply Graz. But it will serve as an example of one of the pleasant little cities of

Slovenia that have no particular attractions of winter sports or mountaineering.

I arrived one morning too early to knock up old acquaintances, so strolled out of the town to the old fortress on the hill nearby. There was no one there, but the main gateway was open and I could pry about inside. It was a typically mediaeval fortified church, in the Gothic style, evidently little used, for the church was bare and chill. Only in the side-chapel a baroque altar clashed with the impression of chivalrous austerity. After a few moments I came out and smoked quietly on a wooden bench opposite a tiny café, also apparently deserted, on whose wall St Florijan, patron of firemen, was depicted pouring water on a burning house. Probably both church and café are only frequented on saints' days. It was getting warm and the air was full of scents and the humming of innumerable bees. Thence I returned past the inevitable Stations of the Cross to Slovenjgradec.

It was on this hill that the temple of Roman Colatium stood, but there were no traces left there, though in the city a few inscriptions and columns are preserved. The castle itself dates from about 1000, and the town of Slovenjgradec – then Windischgraetz, which means the same thing – is first mentioned in documents between 1090 and 1206 as the site of a mint. In 1453 the cure of the parish was entrusted by the Emperor Frederick III to Aeneas Silvius Piccolomini, who later became Pope Pius II. Later in the century Slovenjgradec suffered badly from the inevitable Turkish raids, and in 1489 from the Magyars.

Perhaps its most interesting association, however, is with the famous Austrian family that took its name from the place, Windischgraetz. Their former summer palace still exists, a sprawling building of stucco arcades and many outhouses. It is now a school. Also Hugo Wolf was born here, in an old house on the left of the main street. I was glad to know this. Now I can better appreciate the facile beauty of his songs.

But I had come to see the church. There are, in fact, two. The modern one, built after the Turkish raids, is baroque and uninteresting. The older one was first deserted and then turned into a storehouse. Recently it was reopened and cleansed of its rubbish. It was built in 1251 and dedicated to St Elizabeth. Just before the

Turkish raids – in 1450 – it was decorated throughout in fresco by the painter Andreas of Otting. Twenty-four years later, the church was deserted, with the result that the frescoes have been almost perfectly preserved in all their original freshness. They are perhaps the most wonderful examples of Gothic painting in Slovenia.

But it was time for me to take the train back into the familiar karst and towards the frontier. The few hours I still had before the train left I spent with a young Slovene wandering about the fields and watching the antics of a nestful of young hawks. My companion was learning English by some home-made method of his own. I left Slovenjgradec and Slovenia with his heartfelt farewell in my ears:

'Good-bye, mister; I am afraid to see you again.'

*Mt. Galovec,
Slovenia*

Index